Cables,
Diamonds,
Herringbone

Cables, Diamonds, Herringbone

Secrets of Knitting
Traditional Fishermen's Sweaters

Sabine Domnick

Down East BOOKS

For my mother, Else Solleder,
who taught me how to knit when I was a little girl

For Norah Woodhouse,
who told me so much about gansey knitting

And in memory of Jean Johnson,
who gave me a lot of authentic information,
but died before the completion of this work

English language edition © 2007, original German edition © 2004
by Urania Verlag, Stuttgart, part of Verlagsgruppe Dornier GmbH

English translation by Sabine and Uwe Domnick
For photography, art, and other contributor credits, see page 96.

ISBN (10-digit): 0-89272-688-1
ISBN (13-digit): 978-0-89272-688-2

Printed in China   OGP   5   4   3   2   1

LIBRARY OF CONGRESS CATALOGING-IN-PUBLICATION DATA

Domnick, Sabine.
  [Pullover für kalte Tage. English]
  Cables, diamonds, and herringbone : secrets of knitting
traditional fishermen's sweaters / Sabine Domnick ; English
translation by Sabine and Uwe Domnick. -- 1st U.S. ed.
    p. cm.
  ISBN-13: 978-0-89272-688-2 (trade pbk. : alk. paper)
  1. Knitting--Patterns. 2. Sweaters. I. Title.
  TT825.D66 2007
  746.43'2041--dc22
                         2007027609

Down East Books is a division of Down East Enterprise, Inc.,
publisher of *Down East*, the Magazine of Maine

Distributed to the trade by National book Network
Orders: 1-800-685-7962 / www.downeast.com

Contents

Preface   6

The History of the Ganseys   7

The Fisherman's Sweater   9
  Sweaters with Underarm Gussets   10
  Sweaters with Shaped Armholes   10

Materials, Tools, and Techniques   11
  Yarns   11
  Needles   11
  Other Tools   11
  Preparing to Knit   12
    Check Your Gauge   12
    Casting On   13
    The Ribbing   13
    Joining a New Ball of Yarn   13
    Leaving Stitches   13
    Seam Line Stitches   13
    Selvedge Stitch   14
  Measurements and Shaping   14
    How to Measure   15
    A Word about Measurements   15
  The Sleeves   16
  The Underarm Gusset   16
    Three Knit Stitches as Seam Line   17
    Two Knit Stitches as Seam Line   17
    One Patterned Stitch as Seam Line   17
    Increase along Central Axis   17
  Joining Shoulders   18
    Three-Needle Cast-Off on the Inside   18
    Three-Needle Cast-Off on the Outside   18
    Grafting Shoulder Stitches Together
      (Kitchener Stitch)   18
    Three-Needle Cast-Off with Neck Gusset   19
    Horizontally Knit Shoulder Strap
      (Saddle Shoulder)   19
    Horizontally Knit Shoulder Strap with
      Neck Gussets   19
  Checking the Fit   20
  Legends for Diagrams   20

Illustrated Sweater Knitting Course   21
  Knitting These Sweater Designs   23

Sweater Designs   24
  The Working Sweater   25
  Ladies' Basic Sweater   29
  Gina's Pattern   32
  Sheringham Gansey   36
  Moray Firth   40
  Church Windows   44
  Traditional Gansey   48

The Patterns   52
  Seed and Moss Stitch Patterns   54
  Vertical Textured Patterns   55
  Horizontal Patterns   57
  Vertical Patterns with Motifs   63
    Cables   63
    Diamonds   67
    Herringbone   71
    Zig-Zags   72
    Steps, Ladders, and Bias Lines   76
    Tree of Life   79
    Triangles   82
    Chevrons   84
  Complex Patterns   85
    Filey and Flamborough   85
    Eriskay   90
  More Pictorial Motifs   94
  Initials   95

Yarn Sources   96

Bibliography   96

Acknowledgments   96

Photography and Art Credits   96

Preface

For years I had been knitting for my family following a somewhat old-fashioned book about fishermen's sweaters: Gladys Thompson's *Patterns for Guernseys, Jerseys, and Arans*, which even after nearly forty years is still on sale and highly regarded. Then, with increasing experience, curiosity got the better of me, and I decided to go back to the roots of the phenomenon of Guernsey and Jersey knitting.

I started my research with an inquiry to the Tourist Information Centre of Filey, in Yorkshire, a place repeatedly mentioned in Thompson's book. Filey is a seaside holiday resort and a former fishing village, whose famous fishermen's sweaters were noted in the official tourist brochure.

I had already forgotten that attempt when, after a couple of weeks, I received a big envelope from the Tourist Information Centre enclosing a polite letter readily offering me further help and—what a great surprise—instructions for an original Filey sweater specially written for me with loving care and devotion by the author of the letter. Meanwhile, that initially businesslike contact has developed into a friendship that opened doors and gave me insight into this unique and remarkable knitting tradition.

Just as for more than two hundred years British fishermen's wives have artistically and skilfully created warm sweaters with their busy needles, you also can produce sweaters individually designed and made by you. With some patience and practice, you will progress from simply following a set of instructions to creating original designs showing your own craftsmanship and even real art. For that is what good fishermen's sweaters are—folk art! I would like to show you the way—it isn't difficult at all!

Best wishes for delightful knitting and good success.

—Sabine Domnick

The History of the Ganseys

The pattern on pages 32–35, which I call Gina's Pattern after the person who showed it to me, is a fine example of a traditional sweater passed down directly from knitter to knitter. It is one of those lucky and extremely rare instances where a traditional pattern has carried from the past into the present, kept alive by generations of mothers and daughters.

In 1974, when Gina married Richard, descendant of an old, established Filey fishing family and voluntary member of the lifeboat crew, she decided to provide him with genuine fishermen's sweaters, the garb still preferred by these men except when they have to appear in uniform on official occasions. Thus a centuries-old tradition of British fishermen, which is nearly extinct at most other places, has been kept alive right into the present day by members of the Royal National Lifeboat Institution.

At that time, Mrs. Elizabeth Hunter, who lived on Queen Street in one of the stone fishermen's houses that, unfortunately, have since been cleared away, had already knit numerous sweaters for her husband and other fishermen and was well known for her skills. When she was asked by Richard's grandmother, a former neighbor, to introduce a young woman into gansey knitting, Mrs Hunter was delighted. She readily agreed to show Gina that fading art and thus pass on her experience to the next generation, just as she had learned knitting from her mother, her mother from her grandmother, etc.

Very soon after Gina had finished her first gansey, Mrs. Hunter died. Since Mrs.Hunter's daughter was not interested in knitting, Gina inherited the old steel needles (still treasured and in use today) and Mrs. Hunter's short written notes, and thus the right to regard those patterns as her property, a kind of copyright still respected by the knitters grown-up in that tradition. Not a one of the many sweaters Mrs. Hunter knit throughout her life had been made by following a commercial printed pattern.

By the end of her school days, a girl from a fishing family was expected to be able to knit a sweater for a brother or father, particularly if, for some reason, her mother was unable to do so. At the very latest, once she caught the eye of a particular young man ("when we started courting"), a girl would begin knitting her first sweater. She already would have acquired the basic skills of circular knitting at school and at home by making socks and mittens on a set of four or five double-pointed needles. Now all she must do was transfer this skill from short needles to long ones.

Fishing Communities Mentioned in this book:

1. Bude, with Morwenstow to the north
2. St. Ives
3. Penzance; Sennen Cove between 2 and 3; Lizard southeast of 3
4. Polperro, with Looe to the east of it
5. Great Yarmouth
6. Sheringham
7. Hull
8. Flamborough
9. Filey
10. Scarborough
11. Whitby; Staithes to the north and Robin Hood's Bay to the south of it
12. Newcastle upon Tyne with suburb of Cullercoats; Amble and Newbiggins to the north of it
13. Seahouses
14. Anstruther
15. Arbroath
16. Aberdeen
17. Peterhead, with Boddam to the south of it
18. Buckie
19. Inverness
20. Wick
21. Eriskay
22. Mallaig
23. Campbeltown

In most cases, a girl's mother was her only tutor for making sweaters, because each woman, even one's own neighbor or aunt, protected her knowledge and experience as her personal wealth and property. Knitting instructions only existed in the knitters' minds and memories until the first edition of Gladys Thompson's book appeared in 1969.

Mrs Hunter's notes, written down on pieces of cardboard, had been made for simplifying the placement of the motifs when setting the pattern. Sometimes she also stated the number of stitches and the length of sleeves and yoke, etc. Every pattern element was marked. The last prepared panel of cardboard remained empty.

Elizabeth Hunter's patterns are highly symbolic for Filey fishermen. Simple cables stand for the ropes used on their boats, diamonds for net meshes, horizontal lines for ladders or the many steps that people have to walk from the village high above the North Sea down to their boats on the beach.

Further inspiration and new pattern ideas were acquired "by stealing with one's eyes." In fact, from the second half of the nineteenth century up to the 1960s, there were lots of opportunities to do so, as ganseys were regarded as the absolutely essential symbol of a British fisherman and were worn all the time—with the newest one worn on better occasions and for "Sunday best." Also, during the herring season, large numbers of fishermen from other coastal regions came into the ports and harbors from southern England, Scotland, and even from the Netherlands, where the tradition of specific fishermen's sweaters is also deeply rooted. Along with the herring fleets came the gutters, more familiarly called "herring girls" or "fisher lasses," who processed the landed fish. These were mostly Scottish migrant workers, often from remote islands, and they always brought their knitting with them to be taken out in every spare minute. That mobility of the coastal population was enabled by the rapid extension of the railway lines in the nineteenth century. As a consequence, patterns which used to be typical of certain places were carried on and mixed with other patterns. Such an exchange happened in both directions. Some patterns can even be traced on the other side of the North Sea.

The reason Filey and nearby Flamborough were able to preserve the distinct character of their patterns—alternating vertical panels with cables, motifs, and textured stitches—may have to do with the character of their coastline. It is an exposed, relatively harborless stretch of coast that did not attract the Scottish herring fleets, so the families of the local inshore fishermen were not exposed to other knitting patterns brought in from other areas.

Every year, during the town festival in the first week of July, there is a small but highly interesting exhibition in the Filey Heritage Museum displaying the art of gansey knitting, arranged by the last representatives of that tradition. All the knitters are fifty years old or older, and they all regret deeply that up to now none of them has been able to pass on their knowledge and experience to the next generation.

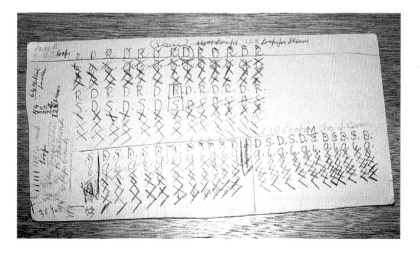

One of Mrs Hunter's cardboard note cards for Gina's Pattern

Fishing vessels at Filey

The Fisherman's Sweater

British fishermen's sweaters are frequently classified as one of two types: Jersey—made from fine wool, and Guernsey—made from medium and thicker yarns. In England this term has been corrupted to *gansey* (or *gansy* in Scotland, where the term is used for any kind of sweater).

We have no clear proof of the connection, but it seems reasonable to assume that these names derived from the Channel Islands of Jersey and Guernsey, especially as the earliest mercantile cottage knitting industry had been established there as early as the sixteenth century, providing sweaters for North Atlantic cod fishermen.

(The Irish Aran Isles sweaters more familiar to American knitters were developed in the twentieth century. Aran knitting is more a modern knitwear fashion and not commonly seen in English and Scottish fishing communities.)

On traditional fishermen's sweaters back and front are identical, so that the sleeves get worn out evenly. A ribbed neckband as wide as the wearer wishes is worked into the neck opening. But if the intended wearer prefers to lay the collar of a shirt or blouse over it, a modern, shaped neck hole with a doubled neckband will be better.

Nearly everywhere in Britain the traditional color of fishermen's sweaters was navy blue. Beginning around 1900 in England gray became popular. In Scotland, natural white was preferred for dressier occasions. In the past green was considered an unlucky color and is still not often seen.

The most characteristic feature of a fisherman's sweater is its knitting process: It is circularly knitted without any seams!

There is a saying among the old knitters from England and Scotland: "Never, ever sew when you can knit!"

Sweaters with Underarm Gussets

Most often in the traditional sweaters, a diamond-shaped underarm gusset was added, which allows the sweater to fit closer to the body while still allowing comfortable arm movement. Half the gusset is knit in the rounds of the front and back, the other half with the sleeve.

1. Work in rounds from cast-on to beginning of armhole.

2. Work in rows to top. Front and back shoulder stitches are joined by being knitted and cast off together—no shoulder seams.

3. Work the neckband.

4. For sleeves, pick up stitches around the armhole and work from top to cuff.

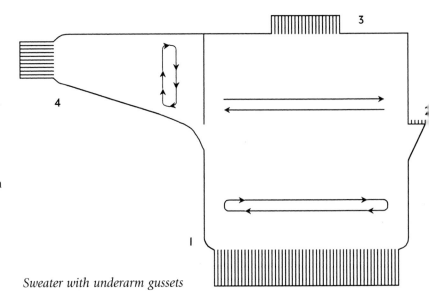

Sweater with underarm gussets

Sweaters with Shaped Armholes

Some fishermen's sweaters are knit with a slightly shaped armhole as we are used to nowadays. This creates a narrower yoke, which looks better on ladies' sweaters. But here, too, the sleeves are directly knit into the armhole without any further shaping of the sleeve top, an ideal way of finding the correct sleeve length.

1. Work in rounds from cast-on to armhole.

2. Work in rows to top, shaping the armhole by casting off stitches while working the first several rows. Front and back shoulder stitches are knitted and cast off together, never sewn.

3. Work the neckband.

4. For sleeves, pick up stitches around the armhole and work from top to cuff.

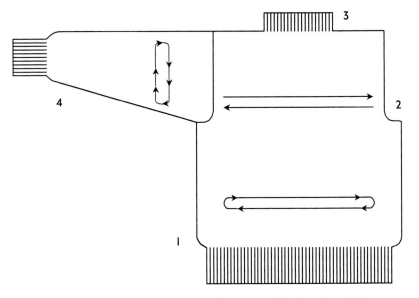

Sweater with shaped armholes

Materials, Tools, and Techniques

Yarns

Classic fishermen's sweaters have always been made from first-quality yarn of pure virgin wool, worsted-spun (with a smooth surface), and very tightly twisted. Formerly, these yarns were produced in 3-, 4-, 5-, and 6-ply, but only the 5-ply is now available. It can be found in good British yarn shops, mainly in coastal towns, or by mail order. The texture of the patterns is shown best with these traditional Guernsey wools, and they are by far the most hard-wearing choice, too!

Wendy Guernsey and British Breeds Guernsey are traditional 5-ply yarns. Evenly spun standard yarns, made from pure wool or wool slightly blended with synthetics, may be substituted. Heilo sport weight, and Brown Sheep Farm's Top of the Lamb sport weight are good choices. Choose yarns with a smooth surface and even color. Many patterns turn out well even with cotton yarns.

The modern yarns that I used for the sweater examples in this book were Schachenmayr Extra and Regia 6- or 8-ply.

See page 96 for information on yarn sources.

> Use only high-quality yarns! Considering the time you'll invest in your sweater, why compromise when it comes to beauty and durability?
>
> Buy a generous amount of yarn; a spare 3.5 oz [100 g] ball should always be left over for later repairs.

Needles

Knitting with the long, double-pointed steel needles used in the past requires practice. The German firm Gustav Selter, Altena still produces them under the brand name Addi, sold in the U.S. by Skacel.

I prefer the Addi circular needles, which are extremely smooth, so the stitches glide effortlessly.

For the ribbing, use needles 1 or 2 sizes thinner than for the rest of the sweater. Test your gauge carefully to determine appropriate needle sizes for the particular yarn you plan to use.

In general, when working with DK weight yarns, you will need:

Size 2 or 3 [3 mm] for ribbing, neckband, and cuffs:

- 24" [60 cm] circular needle for ribbing
- 16" [40 cm] circular needle for neckband
- 1 set of short double-pointed needles for the cuffs

Size 4 [3.5 mm] for body and sleeves:

- two 32" [80 cm] circular needles, one for knitting plus a spare for measuring
- 1 set of straight needles for the rows of the yoke
- 20" [50 cm] circular needle for upper sleeve
- 16" [40 cm] circular needle for middle sleeve
- 1 set of short double-pointed needles for bottom of sleeve

If using Wendy Gansey or British Breeds traditional yarns, use needles one size smaller.

Contrasting threads mark new pattern rounds

Other Tools

- Stitch holders and safety pins for leaving stitches
- Bits of contrasting-color yarns for marking and provisional cast-offs
- Cable needle and crochet hooks in sizes B/1 and C/2 [2.5 mm and 3.5 mm]

Preparing to Knit

Check Your Gauge/Tension

Knitting a test swatch is absolutely essential to ensure that *your* gauge matches the stated gauge in a published pattern. Also, if you create your own designs, a test swatch will help you determine the number of stitches and rows required.

This sample should not be too small; make it at least 50 to 60 stitches wide and about 6 to 8 inches [15 to 20 cm] long, depending on the pattern, so that the repeat is well shown in both directions. A 1.75 oz [50 g] ball

of wool can easily be knit up.

Even for simple horizontal bands, it is very important to knit a large enough test swatch—at least two bands. For an allover pattern mix, the whole length is recommended.

After your swatch is complete, dampen it, lay it out flat, and let it dry completely. Now you can measure with a ruler and find out the number of stitches and rows.

If no multiple of the pattern repeat can be found to exactly fit the desired width of the sweater, the pattern layout will have to be adapted. This can be done in various ways: by adding stitches to a textured panel or by leaving out one or two of them; by adding knit stitches along both edges of a motif panel; or by widening the side panels below the armholes (often knit in seed stitch).

Casting On

The most frequently used cast-on is the **thumb method**, with the yarn doubled around the thumb. (See above right.) Note that the loose end has to be very

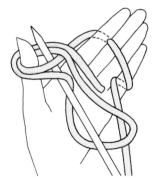

Thumb method: Yarn around forefinger and doubled round thumb. With needle through both loops of thumb, pull thread through.

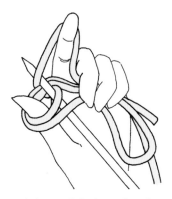

Both loops glide from thumb. Pull thread tightly. Repeat from beginning.

long, to allow 1" [2 cm] per stitch to be cast on. (To play it safe, you can instead attach another ball of yarn, knotting the ends together at the beginning.

For the **knitted cast-on (cable cast-on)**, 2 stitches are cast on conventionally, then add more stitches by inserting the right needle between the previously cast-on stitches, wrapping the yarn around the needle as if to knit, and placing the newly made loop onto the left needle as a new stitch. (See drawings on page 13.)

—Tip—

When casting on, put a bit of contrasting-color yarn after every 50 stitches. This makes counting easier.

Before beginning the 1st round, check that the stitches are not twisted round the needle. Check **again** before commencing the 2nd round!

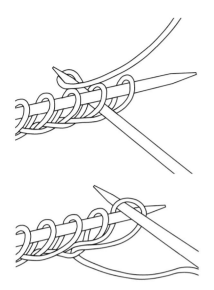

Knitted cast-on (cable cast-on)

The Ribbing

The ribbing should always be worked with thinner needles. For a snug ribbing, you can cast on up to 20% fewer stitches than required for the body pattern. The increase is made in the 1st round of pattern, distributing the increases evenly around.

For a traditional fisherman's sweater, all edges as well as 4 to 6 rounds of ribbing, neckband, and cuffs are worked with a double strand.

Joining a New Ball of Yarn

A new ball of yarn can be attached in various ways.

In rounds: In patterns with 1 or 2 purl stitches lying deeper than their neighboring knit ones, you can knit these purl stitches with both threads, leave the ends on the inside, and darn them in later. In knit sections, you can weave in the thread ends as is commonly practised in multi-color stranded knitting: guide along the end of yarn on the inside and pull through the working yarn—once over and once under, several times. Another possibility is to weave in the ends over few stitches near the seam lines and darn in the ends later.

In rows: Add a new ball of wool always at the edges. Knit the selvedge stitches with both threads and darn in later.

Darning in is always done on the inside with simple stitches, invisible from outside. It is recommended to do this into stitches worked with yarn from the previous ball; if unravelling should be necessary later, the ends will pull out easily.

Leaving Stitches

A large number of stitches, such as for half the body or the shoulders, can be left on circular spare needles of adequate length; up to 25 stitches (neck opening) can be placed on stitch holders; just a few stitches can be held on safety pins.

For the gusset stitches between front and back, it is best to cast them off provisionally with a length of contrasting yarn, which is removed later.

Seam Line Stitches

The sides of a circular-knit sweater should be marked by a distinctive line of stitches so that they are clearly visible. This is important for correctly positioning the armholes. Often, when the sides of the sweater are knit in plain stockinette, these "seam lines" are worked as 1 or 2 purl stitches, or k1, p1, k1, but they may be knit stitches or patterned stitches instead.

When working continuous patterns, the beginning of the new pattern round sometimes can occur on a stitch before the seam line, so that the transition to a new round cannot be seen. Here as well, the beginning of the new round should be marked clearly!

Picking up stitches for the sleeve out of the textured selvedge

Selvedge Stitch

In flat knitting, an even edge can be achieved by purling the first and last stitch of every row, pulling tightly each time. This creates a textured edge that allows the rows to be counted easily. Also, stitches can be picked up more easily from this edge than from the long loops of the commonly used chain selvedge—very helpful when picking up the sleeve stitches.

Measurements and Shaping

In most cases the fit of a personally designed fisherman's sweater has to be customized. But this is less difficult than it may look at first. A well-fitting sweater of the future wearer is very helpful for reference, and so is a measurement graph in the matching size taken from a knitting magazine, preferably one for a sweater with drop shoulders.

The key measurements are:

(a) = width, which has to be doubled for the round

(b) = total length

(c) = length from center front or back to end of sleeve.

The underarm gusset of a fisherman's sweater adds length to the armhole. Its size (number of stitches and length) should be planned beforehand. The number of increases multiplied by 4 is nearly the number of rounds for the gusset; refer to the round/row gauge to calculate how much length this number of rounds will yield. Subtract half of this measurement from the armhole length of a conventional sweater, the result is the length **(e)** of the yoke.

Example (see diagram below right): All figures refer to a men's size medium. In this case, the armhole length **(e)** of a conventional sweater without gussets would be 11.75" [30 cm].

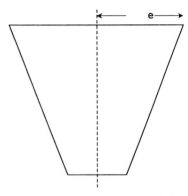

On a flat-knitted sleeve, one-half the sleeve width equals the armhole length.

The gusset requires 8 increases. 8 x 4 = 32 rounds, out of which 31 are knitted, and 31 rounds measure nearly 4" [10 cm]. Half of that is 2" [5 cm]. So, a conventional armhole depth of 11.75", minus 2", equals 9.75" [30 – 5 = 25 cm]. The depth of the yoke knitted in rows **(e)** should measure 9.75" [25cm].

If the sweater body measures a total of 27.5" [70 cm] from ribbing to shoulder **(b)**, the part worked in rounds measures 17.75" [45 cm], and you will begin shaping the gusset at 13.75" [35 cm] from the beginning.

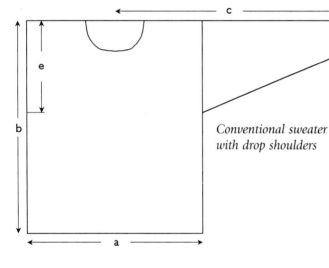

Conventional sweater with drop shoulders

For both types of fishermen's sweater, those with underarm gussets and those with shaped armholes, the length **(e)** of the yoke should be slightly shorter than for a drop-shoulder sweater. The length **(e)** of the armhole is also correspondingly less.

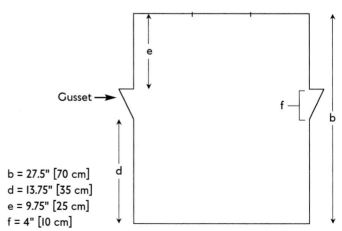

b = 27.5" [70 cm]
d = 13.75" [35 cm]
e = 9.75" [25 cm]
f = 4" [10 cm]

On a sweater with shaped arm-holes, the whole curved armhole edge should not be any longer than the (e) measurement on a conventionally knit sweater. It is easy to make a pattern for the armhole shaping. On a sheet of paper, measure in the desired depth of inset for the armhole, and draw a line parallel to the edge of the paper. Using a firm, non-elastic cord, make two knots separated by the same distance that (e) would be on a drop-shoulder sweater. Now lay the cord along the parallel line, align-ing one knot at the top edge of the paper (= the shoulder line), bending the cord in a smooth curve (shown in red below) so that the second knot aligns with the side edge of the paper. Trace that curved line onto the paper.

By measuring from this pat-tern, you can calculate the num-ber of stitches and rows needed to work the armhole shaping.

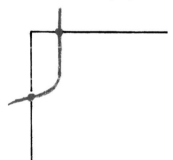

The Neck Opening: For a tra-ditional fisherman's sweater, the stitches at the top edge get evenly divided: always one third for each shoulder, and one third for the neck opening.

For a comfortable shaped neck opening, it is recommended to follow the measurements of a well-fitting sweater or a published sweater pattern.

—Tip—

The yoke portion of a fisher-man's sweater with underarm gussets always turns out to be fairly generous. Therefore, for the same size, the sweater width measurement **(a)** should be up to 2" [5 cm] smaller than it would be for a sweater with shaped arm-holes, or with drop shoulders and no underarm gussets.

How to Measure

Measuring knitwork on circular needles is just as easy as measur-ing one on straight needles. Tem-porarily knit half the stitches onto a spare circular needle of the same size, and your work will lie flat.

Many stitch patterns tend to pull in, so for most accurate measuring, thoroughly wet the knitwork (still on the two circular needles), press out excess water, without wringing, by rolling it be-tween towels so that the needle tips show at the sides. Let it dry completely, lying flat. Now its shape is final and reliable.

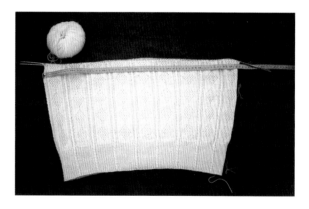

Measuring the knitwork on 2 circular needles

—A Word about Measurements—

The original edition of this book presented all specifications in metric. In this U.S. edition, equivalent values in inches, yards, ounces, and U.S. needle sizes are added for your convenience, but **please note that slight inconsistencies are inevitable whenever measurements are converted.** For example 10 cen-timeters actually equals $3^{15}/_{16}$" rather than 4". The converted meas-urements also have been rounded up or down to the nearest quarter-inch. **For greatest accuracy, measure in centimeters.**

Also, be aware that often there is no exact match between U.S. and metric needle sizes. **Be sure to knit a gauge test swatch,** measure it carefully, and confirm the total stitch count (adjusting needle size, if needed) before you start your sweater.

Stop knitting, dampen the knit-work, lay it out flat, let it dry, and check the measurements at the following stages:

- About 4" [10 cm] above the rib-bing, check the body width.
- Shortly before beginning the gussets or armholes, check the length to underarm.
- After joining the shoulders, when all edges should align so stitches for sleeves and neck-band can be picked up easily.
- Finally, measure the sleeves as you work, to ensure correct width and length.

The Sleeves

Sleeves are directly knit into the armhole and worked from the top downward. The stitches are knit up around the armhole edge after shoulder seams are joined.

To even up the edges and make it easy to pick up stitches for the neckband and sleeves, dampen the fabric, lay it out flat, and allow

to dry, just as you did when check-ing measurements (page 15).

There is no rule for correct sleeve width; this is more or less a matter of experience and personal preference. The following way may be helpful:

1. Measure the yoke length (e) of the knitwork with underarm gussets or the length of the arm-hole edge on a knitwork with shaped armholes.

2. Calculate number of stitches needed to fill that length, based on the gauge of the desired sleeve pattern.

3. Subtract about 10%—this is the number of stitches to knit up around the armhole.

4. As you knit up stitches, make sure they are divided evenly between back and front. If you worked a purl selvedge stitch along the edges of the armhole, you probably will find that you need to pick up 1 stitch in each "knot" and 2 or 3 stitches be-tween "knots."

5. After you have worked about

4" [10 cm], check the width! Knit half the stitches onto another short circular needle so the sleeve can lie flat. Shoulder line and sleeve centerline should form one straight line, without a bend. If the sleeve centerline flares up-ward, the sleeve is too wide; if it tapers downward, the sleeve is too narrow.

The Underarm Gusset

In the old days, the traditional fishermen's sweaters were fairly tight fitting. Diamond-shaped underarm gussets, mostly in plain knit stitches, gave additional ease at the armhole.

At the seam line stitches, in the rounds of front and back, 2 stitches are increased every 4 rounds until the gusset reaches the desired length. From this point on, the front and back yokes are knit separately, working in rows, not including the gusset stitches, which are taken up later when knitting the sleeve.

As the sleeve is worked, the gusset stitches are decreased by 2 stitches every 4 rounds. The for-mer seam line stitches between front and back are continued as the long axis of the gusset and then as seam line stitches of the sleeves, as shown in the photos.

The right decreases are worked as: slip, slip, knit the 2 slipped stitches together (SSK).

Left decreases are worked as: knit 2 together (k2tog).

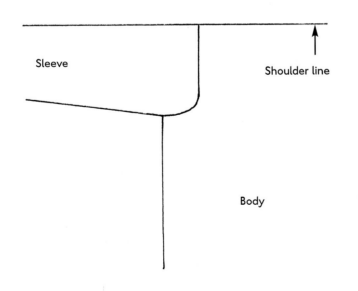

Sleeve

Shoulder line

Body

For the following examples of different gusset styles, a darker color yarn is used for the body and a lighter color for the sleeves. The gussets are outlined with white stitching for clarity.

Three Knit Stitches as Seam Line

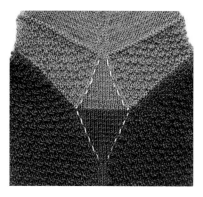

Increase 1 stitch on each side of the middle seam stitch, then work 3 rounds without increase.

Next increase and all following increases (every 4th round): increase 1 stitch between the stitch of previous increase and the outer knit stitch of the former 3-stitch seam line.

The outer seam line stitches become the border of the gusset and then continue as selvedge stitches for the front and back yokes.

When front and back yokes are divided, all the increased stitches and the central seam stitch are cast off provisionally using contrasting yarn, to be later picked up and knit along with the sleeve. The first and last stitches picked up for the sleeve are always knit stitches, and all the gusset decreases are worked inside these marker stitches.

Two Knit Stitches as Seam Line

For the 1st increase, the 2 added stitches have to come between the 2 seam line stitches. Work the rest of the increases every 4th round as described at left. When the gusset stitches are decreased later, the 2 knit stitches bordering the gusset continue on as the sleeve seam stitches, and the sleeve decreases are worked along both sides of this line.

One Patterned Stitch as Seam Line

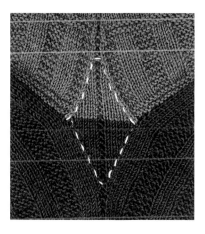

A single-stitch patterned seam line runs between front and back, through the gussets, and down the sleeves. Work the increases as described under "Three Knit Stitches as Seam Line" in left column. Sleeve decreases are worked along both sides of seam line.

Increase along Central Axis

The seam line is formed by a single knit stitch. All increases and decreases are worked symmetrically along both sides of the seam stitch, which also becomes the gusset's central axis.

Of course, these basic schemes can be varied; other gusset layouts can be developed out of the main pattern. If the gusset becomes wide enough before the necessary length is achieved, just add more rounds without increase. When the sweater is worn, such an "offense" will not be noticed at all. On historic sweaters one can often discover instances of "cheating." A design planned with absolute precision beforehand was rare in folk knitting. Hardworking women simply did not have the time—they just knitted.

Joining Shoulders

The shoulder stitches of the front and back yokes may be joined either by casting them off together or by grafting. In the photographed examples the connections are worked in a lighter-colored yarn for better visibility.

Three-Needle Cast-Off on the Inside

This cast-off is nearly invisible on the outside and appears as a single row of chain stitch. Place front and back shoulder stitches onto two identical needles and align the shoulders with right sides together. Insert a 3rd needle through the 1st stitch on both front and back needles as if to knit, wrap the yarn and pull through. Repeat. Lift the 1st knit stitch over the 2nd one and drop it off the needle. Cast off remaining stitches the same way.

As this cast-off is equivalent to crocheted half-stitches, it also can be done with a crochet needle.

Three-Needle Cast-Off on the Outside

This shoulder cast-off makes a more prominent, decorative line that looks good on garter stitch shoulder straps. It is worked the same way as the preceding cast-off, but align the shoulders with wrong sides together.

—Tip—

Joining and casting-off the shoulders can also be done with full crochet stitches: Using a crochet hook, pull the yarn through matching back and front stitches, pull yarn through once more through new and previous stitch. This gives a much firmer shoulder connection.

Grafting Shoulder Stitches Together (Kitchener Stitch)

Worked in the same color yarn, this elegant shoulder connection is completely invisible. The resulting join is equivalent to 2 knit rows.

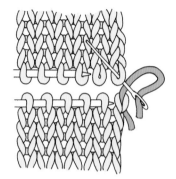

Grafting: Bring the yarn up through 1st stitch on lower needle, then up through corresponding stitch on upper needle (see above). Weave back through 1st stitch, going from front to back this time, then through the next stitch from back to front.

Go through 1st stitch on upper needle again, this time from front to back, then the next stitch from back to front (see below).

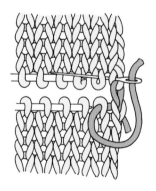

Continue in this fashion, always threading through 2 stitches at a time. Be careful not to pull the yarn too tight.

Three-Needle Cast-Off with Neck Gusset

Inserting a small triangular gusset allows the front neckline to dip slightly lower for a more comfortable fit. For this clever technique, the sweater front and back must be identical. Traditional sweaters often finish the neck opening with a ribbed neckband, as shown in the photo.

Match front and back shoulder, and join by casting off stitches together, working from armhole toward neck, leaving 5 to 8 stitches on each needle. With right side facing, starting with the last stitch remaining from casting off * knit one, turn work; slip 1 stitch purlwise, purl 1 stitch, add another purl stitch from other shoulder

—Tip—

A neck opening with small gussets looks beautiful when made with a crocheted edge rather than a ribbed neckband. Work I round of solid and I round of reverse crochet stitches. This gives more solidity and can be worn with blouses or shirts. It's even nice on cotton sweaters!

side, turn your work; slip 1 stitch knitwise, knit 2 stitches; repeat from * until all shoulder stitches are knit in.

Horizontally Knit Shoulder Strap (Saddle Shoulder)

This highly decorative shoulder strap requires some preparatory work in the last shoulder row of the front and of back yoke. Since knitted stitches are wider than they are deep, the number of stitches needs to be reduced by about 30%; otherwise the shoulder strap will end up wider than the shoulder. So, in the last row of front and of back shoulders, with right side facing: *knit 1, knit 2 together, knit 2, knit 2 together*, repeat to end.

Insert needles into the stitches of front and back shoulders so that both tips are at the same side. From outside of work cast the required number of shoulder strap stitches onto right-hand needle. Turn and work back on inside, either in purl or in pattern. *Purl together last stitch of strap with first shoulder stitch, turn; slip first stitch knitwise, work in pattern over the strap stitches, knit last stitch of strap together with first shoulder stitch by slip,

slip, knit the 2 slipped stitches together (SSK), turn; slip first stitch purlwise, work strap stitches in pattern; repeat from * until all shoulder stitches have been worked.

If the pattern on the strap will continue onto the sleeve, work from neck to armhole. If not, the shoulder strap can be knitted in opposite direction so that at the end its stitches can be merged into the neckband

Horizontally Knit Shoulder Strap with Neck Gussets

Another absolutely clever idea! Front and back are alike. Insert markers in the next to last row, dividing the stitches: ⅓ for shoulder, ⅓ for neck, ⅓ for shoulder. Also mark the last 6 to 8 shoulder stitches on the neck side; these will adjoin the gusset portion of the neck strap (see photo).

In the last shoulder row, reduce the number of shoulder stitches by a third, as previously described under "Horizontally Knit Shoulder Strap." Work the shoulder strap from armhole to neck, either ribbed, as shown in photo, or a pattern of your choice. At the end of each row, knit the last stitch of the strap together with next shoulder stitch of the yoke. The stitches reserved for the small side gussets are not knit in but are added to the strap. All stitches around the neck opening are then knitted up for working the ribbed neckband.

Checking the Fit

Before starting to work the sleeves, try on the sweater to check length, width, and neckband fit. This may save great disappointment later on, if it turns out that the neck or shoulders should be altered. Another try-on is advisable before you start knitting the cuff of the first sleeve.

Remember, even if an alteration should be necessary, unravelling once is never as bad as wearing a badly fitting sweater ever after.

Legend for Diagrams

For Multi-Part Patterns
  A = separating panel
  B = 1st pattern motif
  C = 2nd pattern motif
  Etc.

For Measurements
  Dashed lines mark the sides when knitted in rounds.
  Solid lines indicate selvedges and cast-on or cast-off edges.

For Pattern Graphs

Knit stitches (right side of fabric); purl stitches (wrong side)

Purl stitches (right side of fabric); knit stitches (wrong side)

Twisted knit stitch: Insert needle into back of loop, knit.

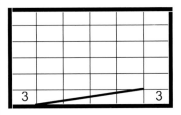

Cable: Slip 3 stitches onto cable needle, put to *front*, knit 3, then knit stitches from cable needle.

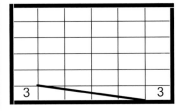

Cable: Slip 3 stitches onto cable needle, put to *back*, knit 3, then knit stitches from cable needle.

Width and length of cable to be adapted to pattern.

Illustrated Sweater Knitting Course

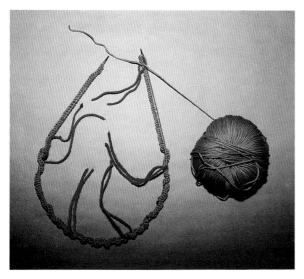

1. With a 24" [60 cm] circular needle, and using either of the methods described on pages 12–13, cast on desired number of stitches, marking every 50 stitches with bits of contrasting yarn.

2. When ribbing is the desired length, switch to a longer circular needle—32" [80 cm]—that is one size larger than used for ribbing. Work increase round, if required. (Increase by knitting into the strand between 2 stitches.)

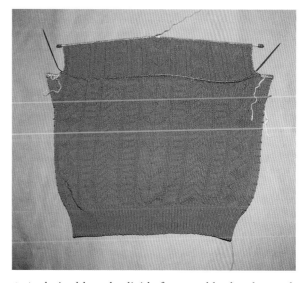

3. Knit up in pattern. In first round, and now and then in later rounds, mark beginning of round with contrasting yarn. Also in first round, establish the side seam lines.

4. At desired length, divide front and back yokes and begin armholes. If gussets are used (pp. 16–17), cast off those stitches provisionally with contrasting yarn. Continue working the back using straight needles; leaving stitches for front yoke on circular needle.

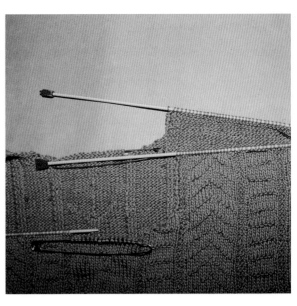

5. When back reaches desired length, place neck stitches on holder and shoulder stitches on shorter circular needles. Transfer front yoke stitches to the straight needles and knit to desired length. Place front neck stitches on holder and shoulder stitches on shorter needles.

6. When front is same length as back, join shoulders using one of the methods described on pages 18–19.

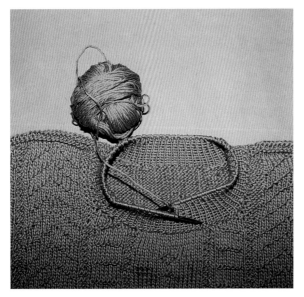

7. Work neckband, using a circular needle one size smaller than used for body.

8. For sleeve, unravel provisional cast-off of gusset (if used), take up those stitches on an auxiliary needle. Knit these first, then knit up the rest of the sleeve stitches around armhole.

9. Knit sleeve with adequate decreases, switching to a shorter circular needle or a set of double-pointed needles when necessary.

10. For cuffs, use double-pointed needles one size smaller than used for sleeve.

Knitting These Sweater Designs

Before you begin to knit any of the sweaters on the following pages, it is absolutely essential to confirm that the sweater measurements are correct for the intended wearer and to study the directions completely and carefully. Refer back to the explanations on pages 14 through 23 as needed. Then you will understand the knitting process and won't encounter irritating hold-ups later on.

When two sizes are given, the figures in brackets are always for the bigger one. If there is only one stated, this applies for all sizes.

The Working Sweater

With a rather unpretentious design, this sweater is similar to the ones traditionally made for everyday work. It is a good introduction to the techniques of Guernsey knitting.

This pattern has been reconstructed from an old photograph from Staithes, in Yorkshire, and it is kept very traditional: circular-knitted, with underarm gussets, seam stitches along the sides, and the wearer's initials above the welt. At hidden places of the upper sleeves I added two motifs I saw on a Northumbrian sweater: heart and cross, the knitter's wishes for luck and God's blessings. Panels in Betty Martin stitch (see p. 54) decorate the armhole edges and shoulder strap of this otherwise plain sweater.

I purposely used a heathered yarn for this sweater. Yarns with some texture or blended colors hide the difference between rounds and rows well on plain knit sweaters.

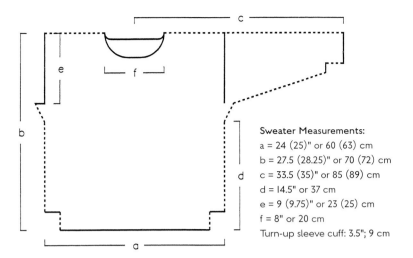

Sweater Measurements:
a = 24 (25)" or 60 (63) cm
b = 27.5 (28.25)" or 70 (72) cm
c = 33.5 (35)" or 85 (89) cm
d = 14.5" or 37 cm
e = 9 (9.75)" or 23 (25) cm
f = 8" or 20 cm
Turn-up sleeve cuff: 3.5"; 9 cm

■ Sizes

Men's L (XL), allowing 4" [10 cm] for ease

■ Yarn and Needles

See p. 11 for information on substituting yarns and choosing needles.

The sweater shown was made with Schachenmayr Regia 6-ply (75% virgin wool, 25% polyamid), total 650 (750) g and 1625 (1875) m, or 23 (37) oz and 1780 (2050) yds.

Size 3 [3mm] needles for ribbing; size 4 [3.5 mm] for body and sleeves

■ Patterns

Ribbing: knit 2, purl 2
Body and sleeves: stockinette (knit on outside, purl on inside)

Betty Martin pattern for shoulders. Row 1: knit. Row 3: knit 2, purl 2. Rows 2 and 4: as stitches appear.
Sleeve motifs: See graphs below.

■ Gauge/Tension

In stockinette stitch, on size 4 [3.5 mm] needles, 24 stitches and 32 rows measure 3.5" [9 cm].

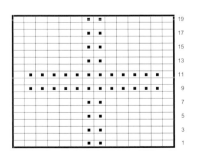

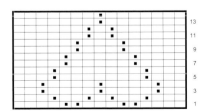

Optional heart and cross motifs

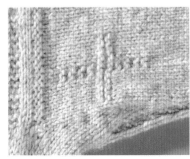

■ Front and Back

Ribbing: Using smaller circular needle, cast on 232 (244) stitches. Work 35 rounds—about 4" [10 cm]—in knit 2, purl 2.

Increase: Switch to larger needle. Working 1 knit round, add 56 (60) stitches by increasing after every 4th stitch, but leaving out the increase 2x (1x). 288 (304) stitches total. Knit 1 more round.

Body: Mark stitches 1 and 2, and stitches 145 and 146 (153/154) to be the seam line stitches; purl these for 2 rounds, then knit them in the next 2 rounds. Work all other stitches in stockinette. At 10 rounds above ribbing, begin working initials, if desired (see p. 95 for alphabet patterns).

Gussets: At 14.5" [37 cm] from beginning, work first increase round: increase 1 stitch on both sides of the 2 seam stitches. Knit 3 rounds. continue increasing 1 stitch on the outer sides of both underarm gussets every 4th round (8 increase rounds total). See the photo on p. 28 and the "One Patterned Stitch as Seam Line" directions on page 17.

Divide front and back: After last gusset increase, work 3 more rounds with no increases. Next round: at beginning of 1st gusset, cast off gusset stitches provisionally with contrasting yarn, work across 142 (150) stitches of sweater back to 2nd gusset and cast off those stitches provisionally using contrasting yarn. Work across the remaining 142 (150) stitches for the sweater front.

Back yoke: Establish pattern panel in 1st row: work 1 selvedge stitch; work Betty Martin pattern for 14 stitches, beginning with 2 knit stitches; purl 2; work across in stockinette to last 17 stitches of row; purl 2; work left Betty Martin pattern panel beginning and ending with knit 2; work 1 selvedge stitch.

At 26.5 (27.5)"or [68 (70) cm] from beginning (Row 3 of Betty Martin pattern) begin working purl ridge across plain knit section: purl center stitches; work back as stitches appear; in next 2 rows, continue Betty Martin panels, knit all stitches in center section. Place center 26 stitches on holder for back neck.

Neck shaping: Working one shoulder at a time and continuing Betty Martin pattern as established, *cast off stitches at the neck edge: 4 stitches, then 3, then 2, then 1. 48 (52) stitches remain.

Shoulder strap: After the neck shaping is complete, begin working Betty Martin pattern across entire width of shoulder. At 20 rows past purl ridge, place stitches on holder. Work other shoulder symmetrically from *.

Front yoke: 1st row on inside of work: Establish Betty Martin pattern panels as on back yoke, work up. At 23.5" (24.5") [60 (62) cm] from beginning, place center 16 stitches on holder for neck opening. Working one shoulder at a time, cast off stitches at the neck edge: 5 stitches, then 4, then 3, then 2, then 1.

Work up shoulder on 48 (52) stitches until it is same length as back (without shoulder strap), ending with a knit row. Work purl ridge for 2 rows, then 1 knit row (outside). Work other shoulder symmetrically.

Join shoulders: Join shoulders by working three-needle cast-off on the inside (p. 18). *For a more elegant shoulder connection:* Without working final knit row on

Initials knitted in above the ribbing

front, graft the shoulder stitches together using Kitchener stitch (see p. 18).

■ Neckband

With smaller needle, knit 26 stitches from back holder, knit up 39 stitches along neck edge, knit 16 stitches from front holder, knit up 39 from other edge, altogether 120 stitches. Purl 1 round, then work 25 rounds—3" [7.5 cm]—in ribbing. Cast off loosely. Fold neckband to the inside and stitch down invisibly on inside.

■ Sleeves

Picking up stitches: Mark center of shoulder. Remove the bit of contrasting yarn from the provi-sionally cast-off gusset stitches and knit those 18 stitches. Knit up 120 (130) stitches around rest of armhole, making sure that center of shoulder falls between stitches 60 and 61 (65 and 66). Altogether 138 (148) stitches.

Patterns: For gusset, continue the seam line stitches as estab-lished, working the rest of the gusset stitches in stockinette. All stitches except for gusset: Purl for 2 rounds, then knit. After 5 rounds of knit, begin working decorative motifs, if desired, plac-ing them on front of sleeve near the gusset, as shown in photo be-low. (Charts are on p. 25.)

Gusset shaping: Decrease in every 4th round, symmetrically to the increase. To the right of the seam line, work SSK; to the left of the seam line, work k2tog. (See p. 16 for more instructions on gussets.)

Shaping sleeve: After gusset shaping is complete, continue decreasing in every 6th round—to the right of the seam line stitches by working SSK; to the left by k2tog.

Cuff: When sleeve reaches the desired length (without cuff), decrease, evenly spaced, to 64 stitches. Switch to smaller needles and work 3.5" [9 cm] in ribbing. Cast off.

Heart motif worked on upper sleeve, near the gusset

Ladies' Basic Sweater

Here's a sweater that is quick and easy to knit, as much of it is worked in plain stockinette. A simple vertical panel emphasizes center front and back, and its pattern is repeated in the shoulder straps. The armhole edges are outlined by two garter stitches.

Using a mottled shade of the yarn hides any uneven stitches that might result when changing from rounds to rows, but if you choose a solid-color yarn instead, the textured panel will stand out more sharply.

Two shining mother-of-pearl buttons hark back to the Scottish fishermen's sweaters with their buttoned neckbands. On those traditional sweaters, the knitter had to be careful to place the buttons opposite the shoulder on which the fisherman carried loads, so the nets and lines (packed in a flat basket called a kishie) would not catch on the buttons.

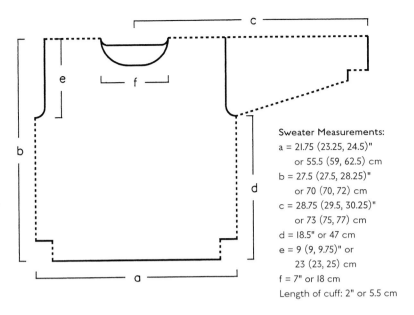

Sweater Measurements:
a = 21.75 (23.25, 24.5)"
     or 55.5 (59, 62.5) cm
b = 27.5 (27.5, 28.25)"
     or 70 (70, 72) cm
c = 28.75 (29.5, 30.25)"
     or 73 (75, 77) cm
d = 18.5" or 47 cm
e = 9 (9, 9.75)" or
     23 (23, 25) cm
f = 7" or 18 cm
Length of cuff: 2" or 5.5 cm

■ Sizes

Women's M/L (L, XL), allowing 4" [10 cm] for ease

■ Yarn, Buttons, Needles

See p. 11 for information on substituting yarns and choosing needles.

The sweater shown was made with Schachenmayr Extra (100% virgin wool), total 600 (600; 650) g and 1500 m, or 21 (21, 23) oz and 1632 yds, in jasper blue, shade no. 3686.

Two .5" [12 mm] mother-of-pearl buttons

Size 3 (3 mm) needles for ribbing; size 4 [3.5 mm] for body and sleeves

■ Patterns

Ribbing: Knit 2, purl 2
Stockinette: In rounds—knit every round; in rows—knit on outside and purl on inside

Textured panel: In rounds—1st round, knit; 2nd round, purl 2, knit 2. In rows—knit on outside; knit 2, purl 2 on inside.

■ Gauge/Tension

In stockinette stitch, on size 4 [3.5 mm] needles, 23 stitches and 32 rows measure 4" [10 cm]

■ Front and Back

Ribbing: Using smaller circular needle, cast on 256 (272, 288) stitches. Work in ribbing for 30 rounds—about 3.75" [9.5 cm].

Body: Switch to larger needle. Knit 1 round, marking stitches 1 and 2 and stitches 129 and 130 (137/138, 145/146) as seam line stitches. Establish textured panel in round 2: Knit 2 seam line stitches; work stockinette for 52 (56, 60) stitches; purl 2, knit 2 for 22 stitches; stockinette for 106 (114, 122) stitches; purl 2, knit 2 for 22 stitches; stockinette for 52 (56; 60) stitches.

Continue as established until piece measures 18.5" [47 cm] or desired length to armhole.

Divide front and back: Work next round to 2 stitches before the seam line stitches, put next 6 stitches (including the 2 seam line stitches) onto a safety pin. Work back in pattern on inside to 2 stitches before the other seam line stitches, put next 6 stitches (including 2 seam line stitches) on a 2nd safety pin. Leave front stitches on needle and begin

working back yoke in rows.

Back yoke: Shape armholes on both edges as you work up by casting off at each end of row: 3 stitches, then 2 stitches, then 1 stitch 6 times. 100 (108, 116) stitches remain.

Now establish 2 garter stitches along armhole edge: knit these 2 stitches on every row.

Neck and shoulders: When work measures 26.5 (26.5, 27)" [67 (67, 69) cm] from beginning, place center 22 stitches on holder for neck opening and commence working 1st shoulder. As you work up, shape neck opening by casting off stitches at neck edge: 3 stitches, then 2, then 2 more. 32 (36, 40) shoulder stitches remain.

Next row, beginning at armhole edge: Work the 2 garter stitches as established, then work rest of shoulder stitches in same pattern as center panel.

Continue in pattern until piece measures 27.5 (27.5, 28.25)" [70 (70, 72) cm] from beginning.

Work other shoulder symmetrically.

Front yoke: Work 1st row on inside in pattern. Shape armhole and establish garter stitch along armhole edge as for back yoke. When front measures 23.5 (23.5, 24.5)" [60 (60, 62) cm] from beginning, place center 18 stitches on holder for neck opening and commence working 1st shoulder.

Shape neck opening by casting off at neck edge: 3 stitches, then 2, then 1 stitch 4 times. 32 (36,

40) shoulder stitches remain.

Work in stockinette, maintaining established garter stitches along armhole edge, until front shoulder is same length as back, including shoulder strap.

Join shoulders: Match up front and back shoulders work three-needle cast-off as described on p. 18. Work other shoulder symmetrically.

■ Neckband

With smaller needle, and beginning at left front shoulder, knit up 31 stitches along neck edge, knit 18 front neck stitches from holder, knit up 40 stitches from neck edge, knit 22 back neck stitches from holder, knit up 10 stitches along neck edge, cast on 7 stitches for button tab: 128 stitches total.

Knit across on inside, trying to continue knit stitches of textured panels so they will merge into the neckband ribbing.

Next row: Work 1 selvedge stitch; purl 2, knit 2 up to the 7 cast-on stitches; 6 garter stitch, 1 selvedge stitch. Continue ribbing for neckband and garter stitch for button tab for 14 rows, working a button hole at rows 5 and 6 and again at rows 11 and 12. (For buttonholes, cast off 6th and 7th stitches after selvedge stitch in one row, then in next row cast on 2 stitches above buttonhole.)

Cast off all stitches. Sew tab end of button band to shoulder. Sew on buttons.

■ Optional Plain Neckband

With smaller needle, knit 22 back neck stitches from holder, knit up 40 stitches along neck edge, knit 18 front neck stitches from holder, knit up 40 stitches along edge. 120 stitches total.

Round 1: Purl, but continue knit stitches from textured panels so they will merge into the neckband ribbing.

Work ribbing for 25 rounds— about 3" [7.5 cm].

Cast off loosely, fold band in half, and sew invisibly on inside.

■ Sleeves

Using larger needle, knit 6 stitches from safety pin, knit up 57 (57, 60) stitches along armhole edge up to top of shoulder, then 57 (57, 60) stitches along other side of armhole. Altogether 120 (120, 126) stitches.

Pattern: 1st round: purl, except seam line stitches. All following rounds in stockinette: knit.

Shaping: Decrease in every 6th round. To the right of the seam line, work SSK for the decrease; to the left of the seam line, work k2tog.

Cuff: When sleeve reaches the desired length (without cuff), decrease, evenly spaced, to 64 stitches. Switch to smaller needles and work 20 rounds, or about 2" [5.5 cm] in ribbing. Cast off.

Gina's Pattern

The pattern of this traditional Filey sweater consists of steps, cables, and diamonds. To read more about Gina's Pattern see p.7.

■ Sizes

Men's M/L (L/XL), allowing 4" [10 cm] for ease

■ Yarn and Needles

See p. 11 for information on substituting yarns and choosing needles.

The sweater shown was made with Schachenmayr Extra (100% virgin wool) in cream, shade no 3502, total 850 (950) g and 2125 (2375) m, or 30 (34) oz and 2325 (2600) yds.

Size 3 [3mm] needles for ribbing; size 4 [3.5 mm] for body and sleeves.

■ Patterns

Ribbing: Knit 2, purl 2
Horizontal ribs (for shoulder

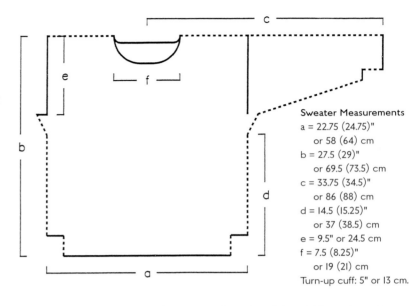

Sweater Measurements
a = 22.75 (24.75)"
  or 58 (64) cm
b = 27.5 (29)"
  or 69.5 (73.5) cm
c = 33.75 (34.5)"
  or 86 (88) cm
d = 14.5 (15.25)"
  or 37 (38.5) cm
e = 9.5" or 24.5 cm
f = 7.5 (8.25)"
  or 19 (21) cm
Turn-up cuff: 5" or 13 cm.

strap): 2 rows purl, 2 rows knit (as seen from outside)

Gina's Pattern (cables, steps, and diamonds): Follow knitting graphs on p. 34.

■ Gauge/Tension

On size 4 (3.5 mm) needles, 1 Gina's Pattern repeat of cable + A + B —33 (35) stitches and 12 rows—measures 4.33 (4.6)" [12 (12.8) cm] in width and 1.25" [3.2 cm] in length. See p. 34 for graphs.

■ Front and Back

Ribbing: Using thinner needle, cast on 264 (280) stitches. Work ribbing for 30 rounds. Mark stitches 131 and 132 (139/140) and stitches 263 and 264 (279/280) to be the seam line stitches. These purl stitches will run continuously from cast-on of body ribbing to cast-off of cuffs; as single purl stitches, they border the gussets and are continued as selvedge stitches along armhole edges of front and back.

Increase: Switch to larger needle and work in stockinette, except for the purl seam line stitches, increasing in 1st round by 64 (72) stitches for a total of 328 (352). *Smaller size:* Increase 1 stitch between knit stitches in all but 2 of the k2 ribs. *Larger size:* Increase 1 stitch between the knit stitches in every K2 rib plus 1

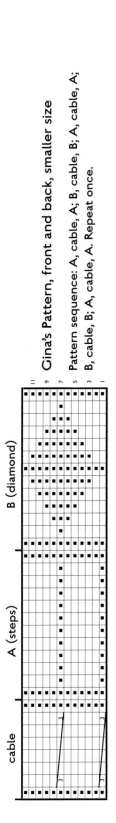

Gina's Pattern, front and back, smaller size

Pattern sequence: A, cable, A; B, cable, A; A, cable, A;
B, cable, B; A, cable, A. Repeat once.

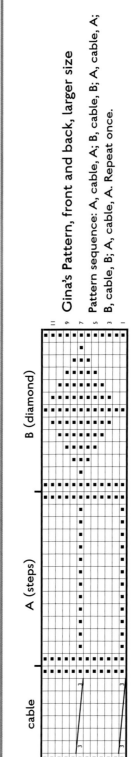

Gina's Pattern, sleeve, smaller size

Gina's Pattern, front and back, larger size

Pattern sequence: A, cable, A; B, cable, B; A, cable, A;
B, cable, B; A, cable, A. Repeat once.

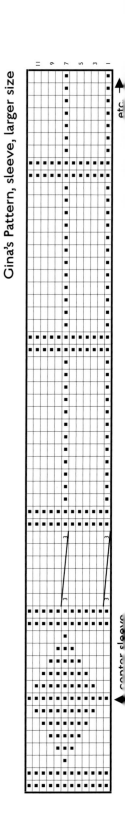

Gina's Pattern, sleeve, larger size

additional stitch on back and 1 on front. Work 1 more round in stockinette, then begin Gina's Pattern.

Body: Beginning with the 3rd round above the ribbing, work the Gina's Pattern motifs according to graphs on facing page. Last stitch of round (purl seam line stitch) is 1st stitch of motif A (steps).

Gussets: At 14.5 (15.25)" [37 (38.5) cm] from beginning, increase 2 knit stitches between the 2 purl seam line stitches. Work 3 rounds without increasing. In next round, increase 2 stitches between the 2 knit stitches previously added. Continue increasing 2 stitches in each gusset every 4th round, always working the increases between the first and previously added stitches. 8 increase rounds altogether = 16 gusset stitches.

Divide front and back: Next odd-numbered pattern round, work to just before gusset at end of round, turn work, and work back in pattern to other gusset. Cast off both gussets provisionally with contrasting yarn. Leave front stitches on spare needle.

Back yoke: 164 (176) stitches. Working in rows, continue up to 19th (20th) pattern repeat. In its last row, place center 30 (34) stitches on holder for the neck opening.

Working one shoulder at a time and maintaining established pattern, complete the neck-edge shaping in the following rows by

casting off 6 stitches, then 4 stitches, then 2 stitches. 55 (61) stitches remain for shoulder.

Shoulder strap: Work in horizontal rib pattern. 1st row: Knit together all 2-purl pairs—50 (54) stitches remain. After working 4th (5th) purl ridge of shoulder strap, leave stitches for 1st shoulder on holder and work the other shoulder symmetrically.

Front yoke: Work back and forth in pattern, 1st row on inside. In last row of 17th (18th) pattern repeat, place center 24 (28) stitches on holder for the neck opening.

Continue working 1st shoulder in pattern, and complete neck-edge shaping in the following rows by casting off 5 stitches, then 4 stitches, then 3, 2, and 1. After 19th (20th) pattern repeat, knit together all 2-purl pairs—50 (54) shoulder stitches remain. Work 1 purl ridge row.

Join shoulders: Match up the corresponding front and back shoulder stitches and graft them together using Kitchener stitch, as shown on p. 18. Work other shoulder symmetrically.

■ Turtleneck

With smaller needle, knit stitches from back holder, in pattern; knit up 43 stitches along neck edge; knit stitches from front holder in pattern; knit up 43 stitches along neck edge—140 (148) stitches altogether.

Work 1 purl round, then 55 rounds—about 4.5" [11.5 cm]—

in ribbing. Cast off loosely in ribbing.

■ Sleeves

Mark center of shoulder. Knit gusset stitches; knit up 137 (145) stitches along edge of armhole, making sure that stitch 69 (73) falls exactly at center mark—153 (161) stitches altogether.

Patterns: Stockinette for gusset stitches; Gina's Pattern for sleeve. After knitting up stitches, set up for Gina's Pattern as you work the 1st round: Purl 55 (59), knit 6 for cable, purl 2, knit 11 for diamond panel, purl 2, knit 6 for cable, purl 55 (59). Next round: Commence 12-row pattern repeats with line 2 of graph. Work 14 complete repeats, then a half pattern repeat with plain knit instead of the diamond.

Gusset shaping: Decrease 1 stitch at outer edge of gusset in every 4th round. The last 2 stitches are decreased by being knit together with the bordering purl stitches. Maintain the 2-purl seam line as you work the rest of the sleeve.

Sleeve shaping: After gusset shaping is complete, decrease 1 stitch on either side of the seam line in every 6th round—to the left of the purl seam stitches by SSK, to the right by k2tog.

Cuff: When sleeve reaches desired length (without cuff), decrease evenly spaced to 64 stitches. Switch to smaller needles and work 5" [13 cm] in ribbing. Cast off.

Sheringham Gansey

Several features of traditional fishermen's ganseys are applied on this sweater: circular, seamless construction; underarm gussets; a historic pattern from Sheringham, in Norfolk; pattern worked only on the yokes and upper sleeves. Two-stitch seam lines run along the body, through the gussets and down the sleeves; worked in knit for two rounds, then purl for two rounds, the seam lines echo the texture of the diamonds in the yoke pattern

Other sweater sizes can be achieved by making the gussets smaller or bigger. (Of course, the number of sleeve stitches would have to be adapted correspondingly.) Making the sweater with a shaped armhole would yield a smaller garment for ladies.

■ Size

Men's M/L, allowing 4" [10 cm] for ease

■ Yarn and Needles

See p. 11 for information on substituting yarns and choosing needles.

The sweater shown was made with Gedifra Shetland (80% virgin wool, 20% alpaca) in cream, shade no. 02, total 900g and 1494 m, or 32 oz and 1634 yds.

Size 4 [3.5 mm] needles for ribbing; size 6 [4 mm] for body and sleeves.

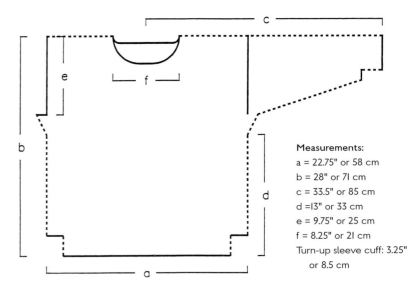

Measurements:
a = 22.75" or 58 cm
b = 28" or 71 cm
c = 33.5" or 85 cm
d = 13" or 33 cm
e = 9.75" or 25 cm
f = 8.25" or 21 cm
Turn-up sleeve cuff: 3.25" or 8.5 cm

■ Patterns

Ribbing: Knit 2, purl 2

Stockinette: Knit on outside, purl on inside

Shoulder strap, horizontal ridges: 2 rows purl, 2 rows knit

Main pattern (diamonds and herringbone): Follow graphs on p. 38.

■ Gauge/Tension

In stockinette stitch, on size 6 [4 mm] needles, 20 stitches and 29 rows measure 4" [10 cm].

■ Front and Back

Ribbing: Using smaller circular needle, cast on 200 stitches. Work in ribbing for 25 rounds or 3.5".

Mark stitches 1 and 2 and stitches 101 and 102 as seam line stitches.

Increase: Change to larger needle. Knit 1 round, increasing 1 after every 5 stitches except at center front and center back and directly before the seam stitches. Altogether 236 stitches.

Patterns: Knit up in plain stockinette, except for the seam line stitches, which are knit in rounds 1 and 2, then purled in rounds 3 and 4.

When body measures 12.5" [32 cm] or desired length, work 2 purl ridges, as follows: knit 1 knit stitch to each side of seam line stitches, purl all other stitches. Repeat purl round. Knit 2 rounds, purl 2 rounds, knit 2 rounds. Then work main pattern according to knitting graph, centering diamond motif at midpoint of front and back.

Gusset: See the photo on p. 39 and the "Three Knit Stitches as Seam Line" and "One Patterned Stitch as Seam Line" gusset directions on p. 17.

In 1st round of main pattern, increase 1 stitch on each side of the seam line stitches, then work 3 rounds without increasing. The 2 knit stitches to the outside of the seam lines will border the gussets and then become the selvedge stitches on the front and back yokes. All further gusset increases are worked inside these border knit stitches as knits.

Continue increasing 1 stitch on each edge of gusset every 3rd round, for a total of 9 increase rounds (20 stitches each gusset).

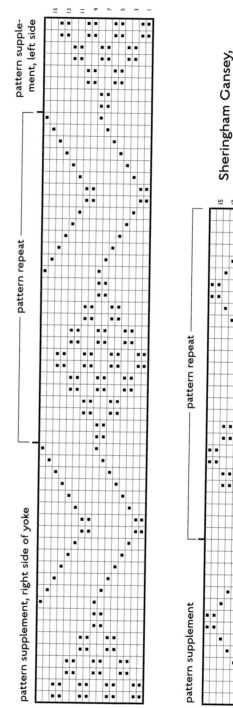

Sheringham Gansey, front and back

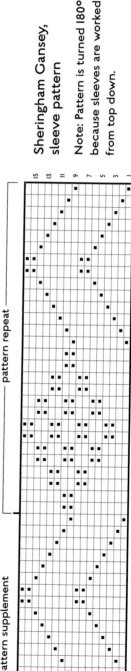

Sheringham Gansey, sleeve pattern

Note: Pattern is turned 180° because sleeves are worked from top down.

Divide front and back: On next odd-numbered pattern round, work to just before gusset stitches at beginning of round.

Work back in pattern, on inside of work, to other gusset. Cast off both gussets provisionally with contrasting yarn.

Back yoke: Leave front yoke stitches on spare needle. Continue working back yoke in pattern, 116 stitches. When piece measures 27" [69 cm] from beginning, place center 20 stitches on holder for back neck.

Working one shoulder at a time and maintaining established pattern, cast off 5 stitches at neck edge 2 times. 38 stitches remain.

Shoulder strap: When you have completed 7 diamond pattern repeats, begin working horizontal ridges (*2 rows knit, 2 rows purl*; repeat * to * once more) for shoulder strap.

Work until piece measures 28" [71 cm], ending with either 1 knit or 1 purl row. Leave shoulder stitches on holder. Work other shoulder symmetrically.

Front yoke: 1st row on inside of work. Continue in established pattern. When piece measures 25" [64 cm] from beginning, place 20 center stitches on holder for neck opening. Working one shoulder at a time, cast off 4 stitches, then 3, then 2, then 1 at neck edge as you work the next 8 rows.

Join shoulders: When front measures same length as back (including shoulder strap), match front and back shoulders and work a three-needle cast-off (see p. 18), inside or outside, just as you like.

(For a less visible shoulder join, graft front and back shoulder stitches together using Kitchener Stitch as shown on p. 18.)

Work other shoulder symmetrically.

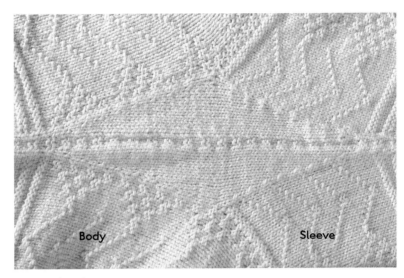

Detail of underarm gusset

■ Turtleneck

Using smaller needle, knit 20 stitches from back holder, knit up 30 stitches along neck edge, knit 20 stitches from front holder, knit up 30 stitches along neck edge: 100 stitches altogether.

1st round purl, then work 40 rounds in knit 2, purl 2 ribbing, cast off loosely in ribbing.

■ Sleeves

Mark center of shoulder. Knit 20 gusset stitches, knit up 100 stitches along armhole edge, making sure that the center falls exactly between stitches 50 and 51. 120 stitches altogether.

Pattern: For gusset, continue knit outline stitches and patterned seam line stitches as established, working the rest of the gusset in stockinette. For the other 98 picked-up stitches: Purl 2 rounds, then knit 2 rounds.

Arrange diamond and herringbone pattern according to graph and work 2 repeats of graph. Work 8 rounds horizontal purl ridges: *knit 2 rounds, purl 2 rounds*, repeat.

Work rest of sleeve in stockinette, except for patterned seam line stitches.

Gusset shaping: Decrease 1 stitch on each edge of gusset in every 4th round, to the right of the gusset by working SSK, to the left by k2tog.

Shaping sleeve: When gusset shaping is complete, decrease in every 6th round, to the right of the seam line stitches by working SSK, to the left by k2tog.

Cuff: When sleeve reaches desired length (without cuff), decrease evenly to 56 stitches. Switch to smaller needles and work 3.5" [9 cm] in ribbing. Cast off.

Moray Firth

This ladies' sweater also utilizes a seamless circular knitting process. It features a traditional pattern from Inverness, running all over from ribbing to shoulder. Small neck gussets enable front and back to be alike, with a comfortable neck opening that, for further solidity, has been given a crocheted edge.

The bigger size is made by enlarging the narrow knit bands to 3 knit stitches instead of 2; this adds 16 stitches to the round. For a smaller sweater than the sizes given here, you can leave out the diamonds along the sides and complete to the desired width with more of the textured columns pattern or plain knit, adjusting armhole position and sleeve width accordingly.

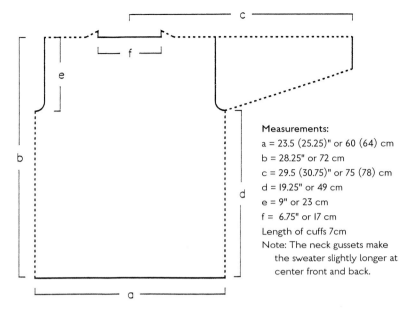

Measurements:
a = 23.5 (25.25)" or 60 (64) cm
b = 28.25" or 72 cm
c = 29.5 (30.75)" or 75 (78) cm
d = 19.25" or 49 cm
e = 9" or 23 cm
f = 6.75" or 17 cm
Length of cuffs 7cm
Note: The neck gussets make the sweater slightly longer at center front and back.

■ Sizes

Women's L/XL (XL), allowing 4" [10 cm] for ease

■ Yarn and Needles

See p. 11 for information on substituting yarns and choosing needles.

The sweater shown was made with Gedifra Shetland (80% virgin wool and 20% alpaca), shade cream no 02, total 900 (1000) g and 1494 (1660) m, or 32 (35) oz and 1664 (1816) yds.

Size 4 [3.5 mm] knitting needles for ribbing; size 6 [4 mm] for body and sleeves

Size E/4 [3.5 mm] crochet hook

■ Patterns

Ribbing. Smaller size: knit 2, purl 2. Larger size: a combination of knit 2, purl 2 and knit 1, purl 1.

Main pattern: Follow knitting graphs on p. 42.

■ Gauge/Tension

On size 6 [4 mm] needles, 1 pattern repeat of 31 stitches (smaller size) measures 6" [15 cm] in width. 1 pattern repeat of 16 rows measures 2" [5 cm] in length. For easier comparison: In plain stockinette, 20 stitches and 29 rows measure 4" [10 cm].

Close-up of main pattern, smaller size sweater

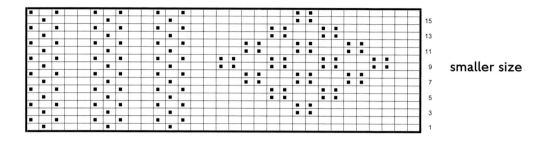

smaller size

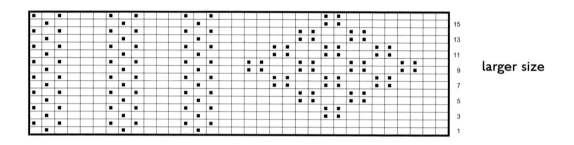

larger size

■ Front and Back

Ribbing: Using size 4 [3.5 mm] needles, cast on 224 (264) stitches and work 20 rounds of ribbing. *Smaller size:* All knit 2, purl 2. *Larger size:* *Knit 2, purl 2 for 18 stitches, ending with knit 2; purl 1, knit 1 for 15 stitches, ending with purl 1*; repeat around.

Increase, *smaller size only:* In knit round, increase 24 stitches as follows, so pairs of knit stitches from the ribbing can be carried through into the main pattern. Knit 19 stitches, *increase 1; (knit 4, increase 1) twice; knit 20 stitches*; repeat from * to * 6 times; (increase 1, knit 4) twice; increase 1, knit 1. Total 248 stitches.

Pattern: Change to larger needle and begin main pattern. *Note*—Pattern begins before the side line, which runs along in the center of the 1st and 5th dia-

mond panels. Work according to knitting graph for a total of 8 pattern repeats plus pattern rows 1 and 2. (For a shorter or longer sweater, adjust number of chart repeats accordingly.)

Divide front and back: When sweater reaches desired length to underarm (here in the 9th repeat), work the next odd-numbered chart row to end; place center 6 stitches from diamond at side line of sweater onto a safety pin; work back on inside to diamond in center of round, at other side line of sweater; place 6 center stitches from that diamond onto another holder.

Back or front yoke: For armholes, cast off on both edges as you work the next 12 rows: 3 stitches, 2 stitches (twice), 1 stitch (3 times). *Larger size only:* Cast off 1 more stitch at each end of 9th row. 98 (104) stitches remain. Work up as many complete pat-

tern repeats as possible, plus pattern rows 1 and 2.

Shoulder strap and neck edge: Maintain stitch pattern for textured columns, but switch to ribbing over diamond panels. (See bottom photo on p. 43.) Work 10 rows of combined ribbing and textured columns. Work other yoke the same, beginning with an inside row.

Join shoulders and work neck gussets: See p. 18, "Three-Needle Cast-Off with Neck Gusset." Match front and back shoulders with right sides together. Starting from armhole edge, cast off together 27 (30) stitches, turn work to outside. Work neck gusset as described on p. 18 until there are 13 gusset stitches; leave stitches on needle and break yarn.

Work other side symmetrically, but do not break yarn; instead, cast off all neck stitches in 1 round. Work 1 round of single

Detail of neck gusset

crochet stitches and then 1 round in reverse (from left to right) around edge, trying to keep the crocheted edge narrow.

■ Sleeves

Knit 6 stitches from safety pin, marking stitches 3 and 4 as the sleeve seam line stitches. Knit up 106 stitches around armhole edge, making sure that centerline of

shoulder falls between picked-up stitches 53 and 54. Altogether 112 stitches.

Pattern: 1st round: Knit the 2 seam line stitches, otherwise purl. Rounds 2 and 3: Knit 34 (32), work textured column pattern for 13 (15) stitches, knit 18 stitches for diamond panel, work textured column pattern for 13 (15), knit 34 (32). Work as many complete

repeats of diamond pattern as possible, then just knit the stitches of the diamond panel.

Shaping sleeve: Decrease in every sixth round. To the right of the seam line stitches, decrease by working SSK; to the left, by working k2tog.

Cuff: When sleeve reaches desired length (without cuff), decrease evenly spaced to 56 stitches. Switch to smaller needles and work knit 2, purl 2 ribbing for 20 rounds. Cast off in ribbing.

Detail of neck and shoulder ribbing and neck edge

Church Windows

This pattern name refers to the small diamond-shaped panes often seen in English and Scottish church windows. In Scotland many variations of this pattern were knitted.

Worked in a fine merino wool, it looks quite elegant and makes a sweater that's perfect to wear over a blouse on a chilly summer evening.

The sleeves, knit in a continuous diamond pattern, stand out against the main pattern of the body. On the body, the cable motifs extend into the ribbing.

The front and back of this sweater are identical, and small side gussets make a comfortable neck opening, which is reinforced by 2 crocheted rounds.

■ Sizes
Women's L (L/XL), allowing 4" [10 cm] for ease

■ Yarn and Needles
See p. 11 for information on substituting yarns and choosing needles.

The sweater shown was made with Schachenmayr Merino (100% virgin wool), in cream shade no. 02, total 650 (700) g and 2080 (2240) m, or 22.75 (24.5) oz and 2275 (2450) yds.

Size 1 or 2 [2.5 mm] knitting needles for ribbing; size 2 or 3 [3 mm] for body and sleeves.

Size B/1 [2.5 mm] crochet hook.

■ Patterns
Ribbing, body: Knit 1, purl 1, alternating with the 8-stitch cable motif from main pattern

Ribbing, sleeve: Knit 1, purl 1

Main pattern: Follow knitting graph on p. 46. Cable twist in every eighth round/row

Sleeve pattern: Use only diamonds portion of pattern graph, without cables

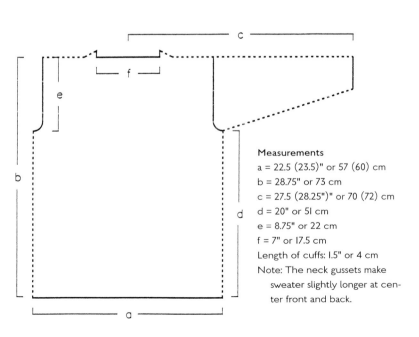

Measurements
a = 22.5 (23.5)" or 57 (60) cm
b = 28.75" or 73 cm
c = 27.5 (28.25")" or 70 (72) cm
d = 20" or 51 cm
e = 8.75" or 22 cm
f = 7" or 17.5 cm
Length of cuffs: 1.5" or 4 cm
Note: The neck gussets make sweater slightly longer at center front and back.

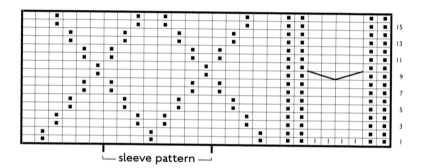

— sleeve pattern —

■ Gauge/Tension

In stockinette, on larger needles (size 2 or 3), 30 stitches and 40 rows measure 4" [10 cm]. 1 pattern repeat, 27 stitches, measures 3.25" [8.5 cm] in width.

■ Front and Back

Note: The pattern repeat begins before the side seam line.

Ribbing and cables: Using smaller needle, cast on 356 (378) stitches. *Smaller size:* *Knit 1, purl 1 ribbing for 35 stitches; [purl 2, knit 4, purl 2 (for cable); ribbing for 19 stitches] x 5; purl 2, knit 4, purl 2 (for cable); repeat from *. *Larger size:* *Purl 2, knit 4, purl 2 (for cable); knit 1, purl 1 ribbing for 19 stitches; repeat from *. *Both sizes:* Make 1st cable twist in 5th round. Work ribbing and cables for 26 rounds.

Pre-pattern rounds: Work 2 more rounds, continuing the cables and their flanking purl stitches as established, but knitting all other stitches.

Main pattern: Change to larger needle. With next cable-twist round, begin main diamonds pattern. For smaller size, adapt diamond pattern to fit the 35 stitches of the side panels.

Divide front and back: When sweater measures 20" [51 cm], work across to just past beginning of round. Place 7 (8) stitches along side line onto a safety pin for beginning of armhole; work back in pattern on inside of work to opposite side of sweater, place 7 (8) stitches along sideline onto a safety pin for beginning of second armhole.

Yoke: Work back and forth in pattern. Shape armholes in following rows: Cast off 3 (2)

stitches at each edge, then 2 (2) stitches, then 1 (1), then 0 (1). Then decrease 1 stitch at each end of every 4th row 7 (9) times. 145 stitches remain.

When piece measures close to 27.5" [70 cm], end the diamonds pattern at a full or half-repeat (after pattern row 10 or 2), but maintain the established 8-stitch cables pattern as you work 2 more rows in stockinette. Switch to thinner needle and work 10 rows of ribbing. Leave all stitches on

Detail of neckband

Detail of neck gussets

needle and break the yarn. Work other yoke the same, but do not break the working yarn.

Join shoulders and work neck gussets: See p. 18, "Three-Needle Cast-Off with Neck Gussets." Match shoulders with right sides together. Cast off together 36 stitches of first shoulder. Turn work to outside.

With the last stitch left, work neck gusset in ribbing, knitting in from each shoulder 10 stitches.

Work other side the same, then knit 1 round of ribbing around all stitches and cast off. Work 1 round of single crochet, then and 1 round of reverse (from left to right) along edge.

■ **Sleeves**

Knit 7 (8) stitches from holder, the stitch(es) in the middle is (are) the seam line stitch(es) of the sleeve. Knit up 137 (143) stitches along armhole edge, making sure that stitch 69 (72) falls exactly at center of shoulder. Altogether 144 (151) stitches.

1st round: seam stitch(es) knit, all others purl. 2nd and 3rd rounds: knit.

Pattern: Begin sleeve pattern in 4th round, centered symmetrically from shoulder line. *Smaller size:* Knit seam stitch, *knit 7, purl 1, repeat from * to end of round. *Larger size:* Knit seam stitches, knit 2, * purl 1, knit 7,

repeat from * to last 2 stitches, knit 2. Fit in as many whole diamonds as possible, reducing the number of diamonds as the sleeve tapers toward the cuff.

Shaping sleeve: Decrease in every 6th round. To the right of the seam stitch(es), decrease by working SSK; to the left of seam line, by working k2tog.

Cuff: When sleeve is desired length (without cuff) end pattern at full or half pattern repeat, then work 2 knit rounds. Decrease evenly spaced to 68 stitches.

Switch to smaller needles and work knit 1, purl 1 ribbing for 20 rounds (2 inches or 5 cm). Cast off in ribbing.

Traditional Gansey

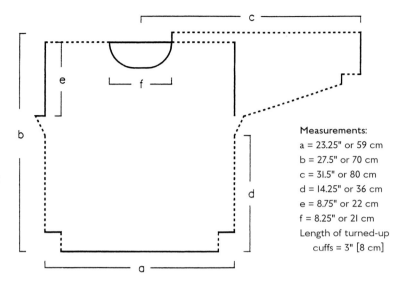

Measurements:
a = 23.25" or 59 cm
b = 27.5" or 70 cm
c = 31.5" or 80 cm
d = 14.25" or 36 cm
e = 8.75" or 22 cm
f = 8.25" or 21 cm
Length of turned-up
  cuffs = 3" [8 cm]

Several features of classic ganseys appear in this interesting but not really difficult sweater. It is circular knit with underarm gussets. The patterns are widespread along the British coasts. The cable of the smart, horizontally knit shoulder strap runs the length of the sleeve.

For a bigger sweater, enlarge the side panels by 4 stitches each (or a multiple of 4), so that the cable pattern can be maintained in the bottom band. Remember that when the body of the sweater is made wider, the shoulder width will have to be adjusted too.

To make a smaller sweater, replace the drop-shoulder with a shaped armhole that omits the whole moss texture side panel.

■ Size

Men's L, allowing 4" [10 cm] for ease

■ Yarn and Needles

See p. 11 for information on substituting yarns and choosing needles.

The sweater shown was made with Gedifra Shetland (80%wool, 20% alpaca) in cream, shade no. 02, total 1000g and 1660 m, or 35 oz and 1810 yds.

Size 4 [3.5 mm] needles for bottom band, neckband, and cuffs; size 6 [4 mm] for body and sleeves.

■ Patterns

Bottom band: mixed cables
Body: cables, diamonds, herringbone, and moss texture panels
Sleeves: cable, moss texture, stockinette
Neckband, cuffs: mini cables
For all patterns, see the graphs on p. 50.

■ Gauge

On size 6 [4 mm] needles. 1 cable and 1 motif panel (= 23 stitches) measure 4" [10 cm]; the length of a diamond (= 24 rows) is 3" [8 cm]. For easier comparison, in stockinette, 20 stitches and 29 rows measure 4" [10 cm].

■ Front and Back

Bottom band: With smaller needle, cast on 240 stitches. Work mixed cables pattern according to knitting graph for the bottom band, making 1st cable twist in 8th round. Total 27 rounds.

Increase and pre-pattern rounds: Switch to larger needle.

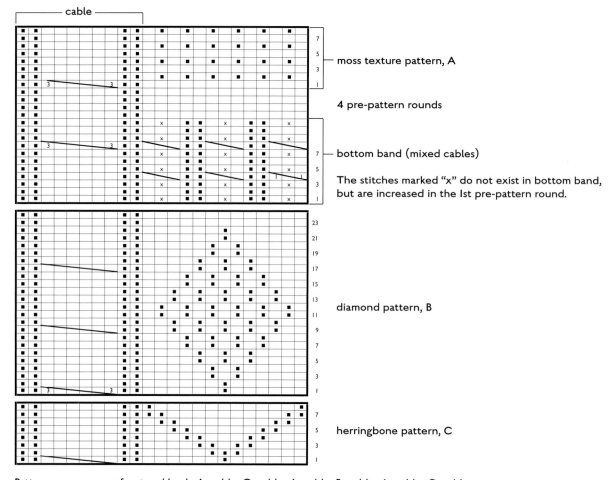

Pattern sequence on front and back: A, cable, C, cable, A, cable, B, cable, A, cable, C, cable; repeat

1st pre-pattern round: Continue large cables as established, knit all other stitches, increasing 1 stitch above each mini cable. Altogether 276 stitches. Knit 3 more rounds, continuing large cables.

Begin patterns and seam line: With next twist of cables, arrange pattern sequence according to knitting graph, with beginning of round falling at center knit stitch of 1st moss texture panel A. Mark 1st stitch of round as the seam line. Work until piece measures 14.25" [36 cm] from beginning.

Gussets: Refer to the p. 17 instructions for a gusset worked above 3 knit stitches. Increase 1 stitch on each side of the seam stitch, then work 3 rounds without increase; increase again on each side of the seam stitch. Continue increasing every 4th round, making all further increases between the 1st and last increases. Altogether 8 increases.

Divide front and back: On the next odd-numbered pattern round, stop just before the gusset at beginning of round and work back in pattern on inside of work to gusset on opposite side. Cast off both gussets provisionally with contrasting yarn.

Back yoke: Leave front stitches. Work in pattern (137 stitches) until back measures 26.75" [68 cm]. Divide and leave on spare needles: 46 stitches for shoulder, 45 stitches for neck opening, 46 stitches for shoulder. Work 1 more row on each shoulder, decreasing 13 stitches evenly spaced, so 33 stitches remain. Leave stitches on holder.

Front yoke: Starting with an inside row, work up in pattern (137 stitches). When front measures 23.5" [60 cm], place center 19 stitches on holder for neck opening and work shoulders one

50

at a time. Continue shaping neck opening in subsequent rows by casting off a total of 13 stitches along neck edge: 4 stitches, then 3, then 2, 2, 1, and 1. When front shoulder is same length as back, work last row with decreases as for back shoulder. Work other shoulder symmetrically.

■ Shoulder Strap

Pick up shoulder stitches on needles so that the tips are at neck side. Following the directions on p. 19, work horizontal shoulder strap over 12 stitches. *Pattern, from outside:* edge stitch, 2 stitches purl, knit 6 for cable, purl 2, edge stitch. Leave stitches on holder when finished. Work other side symmetrically.

■ Neckband

Using smaller needle, knit 45 stitches from back holder, knit up 27 stitches along neck edge, knit 19 stitches from front holder, knit up 27 stitches. Altogether 118 stitches. Purl 1 round, then knit 2 rounds, decreasing 2 stitches in each round by knitting together 2 stitches where the shoulder straps

Detail of underarm gusset

meet the back neckline on each side. 112 stitches remain.

Work 23 rounds in knit 2, purl 2, with mini cable twists in every 4th round. Work 2 rounds of knit.

Cast off loosely. Fold neckband to inside and sew.

■ Sleeves

Remove contrasting yarn and knit gusset stitches, knit up 46 stitches along armhole edge, knit in pattern 12 stitches from shoulder strap, knit up 46 stitches from armhole edge. Altogether 121 stitches.

Pattern: Knit all gusset stitches. Continue cable according to pat-

tern in shoulder strap. In 1st round purl all knit-up stitches; in 2nd round establish moss texture panels along both sides of cable: 13 stitches of moss texture + 2 purl stitches along outer edge of moss panel. All other sleeve stitches knit.

Gusset: Work first and last of the knit-up stitches as moss stitches; they border the gusset, and together with the last remaining stitch from the gusset, they will continue as sleeve seam line stitches. Decrease gusset by 2 stitches in every 4th round—on the right edge by working SSK, on the left by working k2tog.

Shaping sleeve: After gusset shaping is complete, continue decreasing in every 6th round—to the right of seam line, by working SSK; to the left by k2tog.

Cuff: When sleeve reaches desired length (without cuff), decrease, evenly spaced, to 56 stitches. Switch to smaller needles and work 24 rounds in mini cable pattern, crossing cables in every 4th round. Cast off.

Shoulder strap detail

The Patterns

There are only three basic "building blocks" used for creating the infinite variety of patterns one sees in most fishermen's sweaters: knit and purl stitches and simple cables. (On the Hebrides, openwork patterns and the so-called Indian corn stitch are added.) It is endlessly fascinating to see what can be made from just three ingredients which are moved about in vertical and horizontal directions.

Unfortunately, the traditional patterns were written down only fairly late, when the culture of the fishermen's sweaters was already disappearing for various reasons, i.e. decline of the fishing industry, new leisure habits of the women, availability of new textiles, etc. Most authors who dealt with the subject were hobby knitters—though highly devoted and motivated ones—and their private means were limited, so they could record knitting patterns from only certain areas. Inevitably, the selection of patterns presented in these pages can be only a fraction of what has been produced already and of what is actually possible.

Moreover, the patterns shown here should not be considered as absolute and sacred; rather, they are offered to serve as guidelines and as a basis for your own creative designs. By devising your own combinations of the patterns I offer on pages 54–95, you will still be following tradition, for the knitters of the past, too, played with the possibilities and inspirations they were offered. And every folk tradition can only survive when it is dealt with in a creative manner and adapted to the conditions of life for each new generation.

In former times, patterns were only applied on the yokes of

The crew of a Scottish herring boat, late nineteenth century

sweaters, where the thicker texture provided more warmth for the upper torso. The lower parts of the front and back, as well as most of the sleeves, were kept plain; this saved time and yarn and made it easier to repair worn-out garments.

Allover patterns are probably a much more recent phenomenon and were most likely to be seen when the knitter intended to demonstrate her skills, e.g. on a festive-occasion sweater. In some places, young women would knit up a "bridal shirt"—a highly elaborate, skilfully made sweater that she presented to her future husband on their wedding day— to prove her qualifications for marriage.

Most of the motifs are basic geometric constructions consisting of purl stitches arrayed on a plain knit background. Twisted cables add more depth to the patterns. This principle of design can be found in many ethnic traditions of needlework and other crafts.

The names of the motifs were given later and were derived from the people's everyday life and environment. Sometimes symbolic and religious meanings were added.

Cables represent ropes used on ships, **diamonds** represent the meshes of a fishing net. **Herringbone** stands for a fisherman's catch and thus for success in one's career.

Zig-zag is sometimes called "flash of lightning" or "path in

Jane Marks with her knitting, above the cliffs of Polperro, Cornwall, in the second half of the nineteenth century

the cliffs"; a double zig-zag is called "marriage lines," an allusion to the ups and downs in married life.

Steps and ladders portray the steps and ladders found on board ships and in the ports; in some places, a wide ladder motif is called "Jacob's ladder," a Biblical image.

The **tree of life** motif means good wishes for the life of the wearer and his family. Triangles represent nautical signal **flags**.

Pictorial motifs are **heart, anchor,** and **cross**. The heart symbolizes the knitter's love for the wearer, of course. The anchor wishes the wearer a safe journey, and the cross represents God's blessings.

Initials were knitted in to identify the numerous, mostly similar

sweaters worn by members of large fishing families.

All patterns presented in the following pages are traditional. I've collected them from publications, from sweaters in museums, and from sweaters made by still active knitters or reconstructed from old photographs. They are roughly ordered according to their most prominent motifs, but crossovers cannot be avoided, as only a few are purebred. Some of the patterns have been slightly adapted for easier knitting.

Seed and Moss Stitch Patterns

These basic patterns can be used in various ways to add texture in the yoke of an otherwise un-patterned sweater: in horizontal "banded patterns," as narrow vertical separators between motifs, in wider vertical panels, or to fill in motifs such as diamonds.

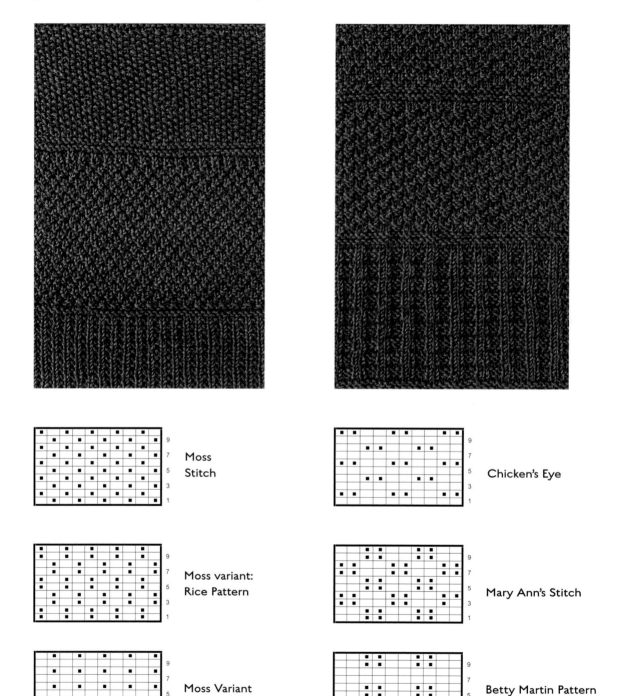

Moss Stitch

Chicken's Eye

Moss variant: Rice Pattern

Mary Ann's Stitch

Moss Variant

Betty Martin Pattern

Vertical Textured Patterns

Pattern from Flamborough

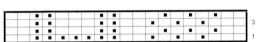

Pattern from Filey

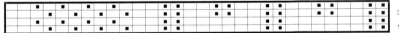

Pattern from Fife

Two Patterns from Seahouses, Northumberland

Miss Esther Rutter's Pattern

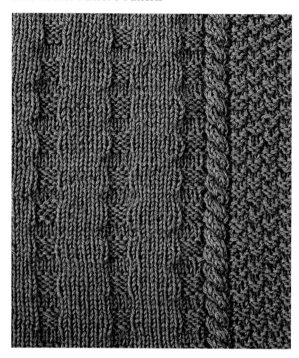

Wide textured panel in center, flanked by cables and side panels in Mary Ann's stitch

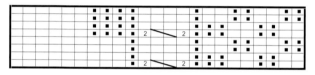

Wave Pattern, Seahouses

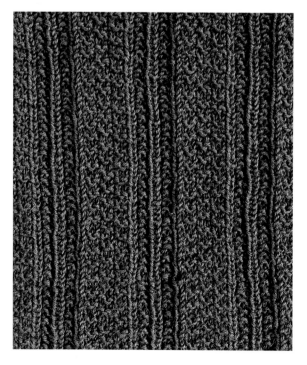

Horizontal Patterns

Stephen Hawker's Slate Pattern, Morwenstow

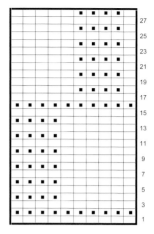

Stephen Hawker (1803–1875), vicar at Morwenstow in Cornwall, was a poet and a rather eccentric person. He called himself a "fisher of men" and always wore fishing boots and a hand-knit fisherman's sweater in order to show solidarity with his flock of fishing folk, in spite of his constant railing against their smuggling activities.

Construction schemes for horizontal patterns (or "banded patterns")

The letter A stands for a repeated separating band between design panels. Read from bottom to top.

A	A
D	B
A	A
B	B
A	A
C	B
A	A
B	*Example:* Lizard lattice pattern
A	(p. 62, top photograph)

Example: Banded pattern from Newhaven, shown at right.

All horizontal patterns can work for shoulder straps, which are an important design feature of fishermen's sweaters. Shoulder straps also allow you to make up the needed additional length depth when a pattern repeat ends short of the desired total length to shoulder.

Horizontal pattern from Newhaven, the earliest known photograph of a fisherman's sweater.

Newhaven Pattern

6-stitch pattern repeat + 4 stitches + 2 selvedge stitches.

When working in rows, purl all wrong-side (even-numbered) rows.

Rows 1, 3, 5: Knit 4, slip 2 stitches purlwise; repeat; end with 4 knit.

Rows 7, 9, 11: Knit 1, slip 2 stitches purlwise, * knit 4, slip 2 purlwise *, repeat from * to *; end with 1 knit.

Repeat 12 rows of pattern to desired depth of band.

Pattern from the Heritage Museum of Newhaven, near Edinburgh

Adjust depth of bands as desired.

Yoke Pattern of the Northcott Family, Polperro

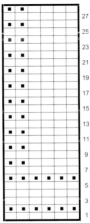

Norfolk Pattern

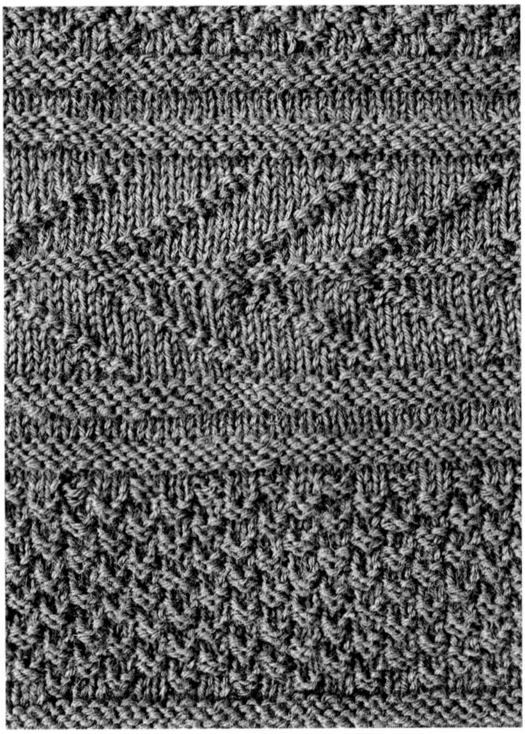

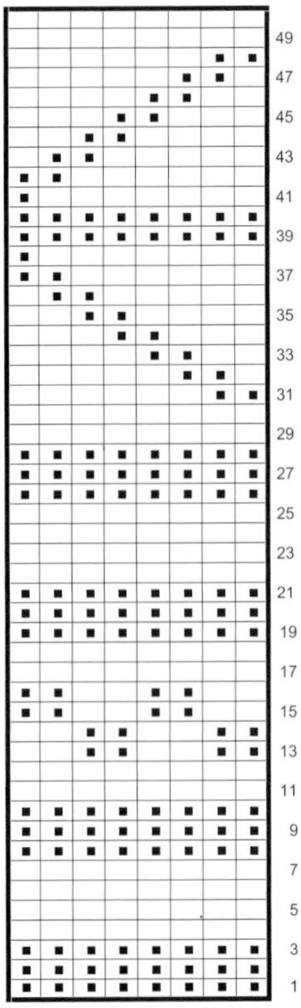

Adjust depth of bands as desired.

Pattern from Cullercoats

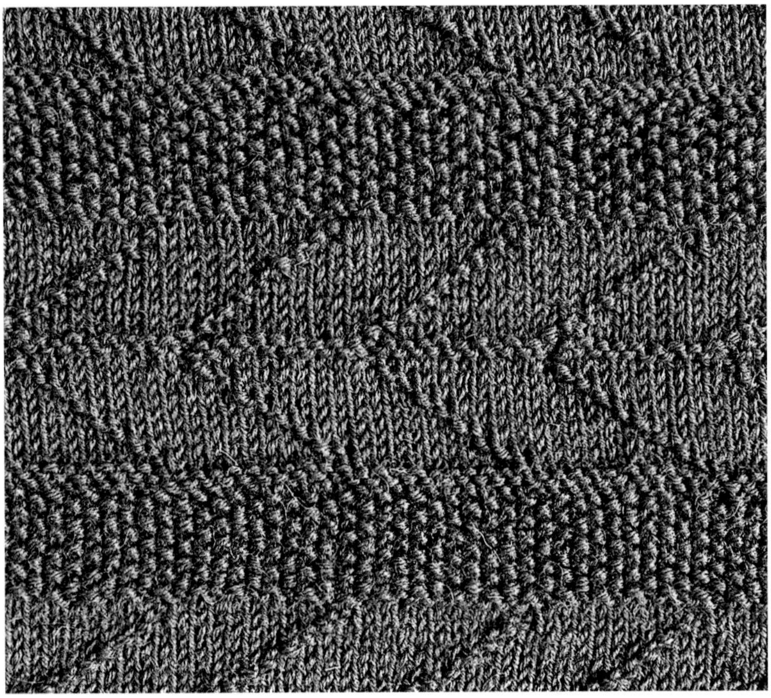

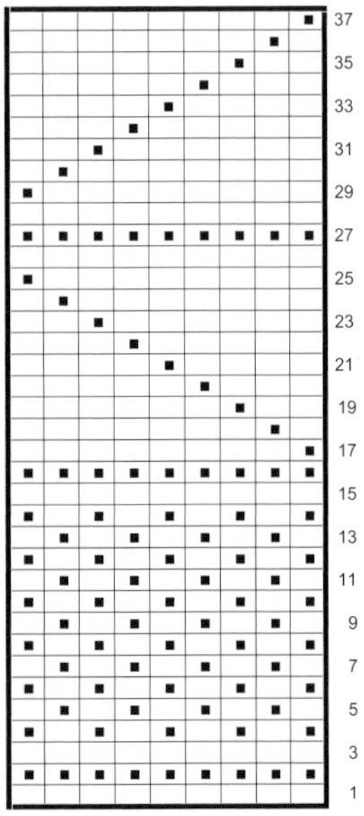

Scottish Fleet Pattern A

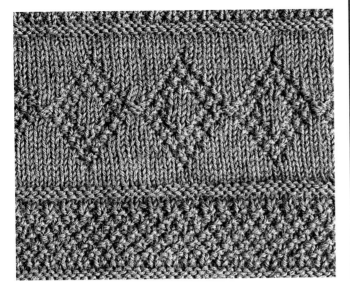

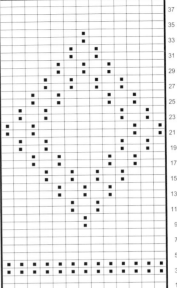

Scottish Fleet Pattern B

Lizard Lattice Pattern

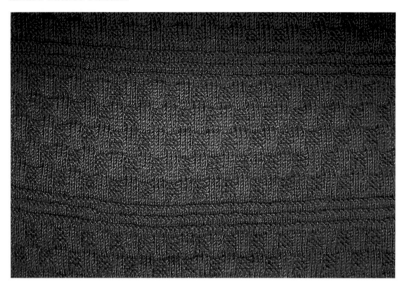

Chicken's Eye Pattern, Staithes

This extremely popular pattern was knit all along the British coasts and even in the Netherlands and Germany. Sometimes it was worked with 3 purl stitches instead of 2, and quite often, the horizontal separating ridges were varied.

Vertical Patterns with Motifs—Cables

Buckie Cable Pattern

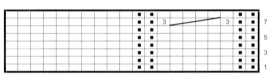

Scilly Isles Pattern

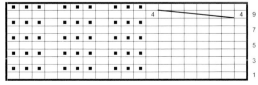

Ribs and Cable Pattern, Campbeltown

Such cable rib variations were always knit with a moss shoulder strap.

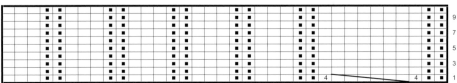

Staithes Pattern A

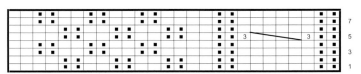

Staithes Pattern B

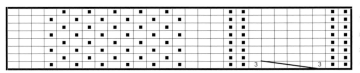

Cullercoats Pattern

On the original sweater it was used in the yoke only, separated from the plain part by horizontal bands, as shown on p. 60.

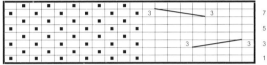

Horseshoe Cable and Steps, Filey (Jean Johnson)

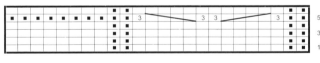

Snake Cable, Polperro

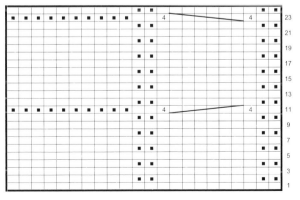

Mrs Redford Armstrong's pattern, Amble, about 1980

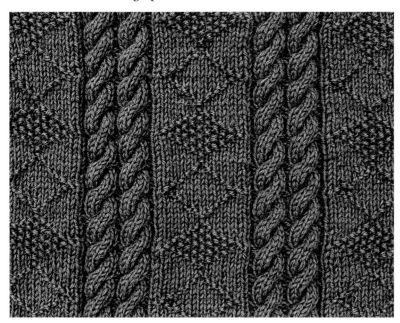

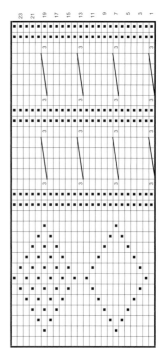

Wick Pattern

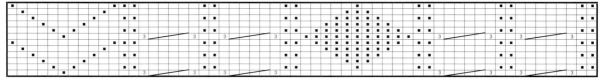

Vertical Patterns with Motifs—Diamonds

Moss Diamonds and Herringbone, Sheringham

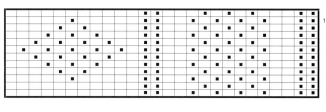

Moss Panels and Diamonds, Filey

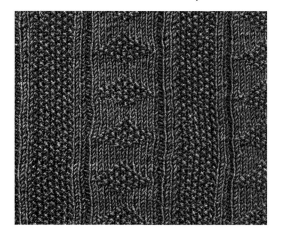

Net Pattern

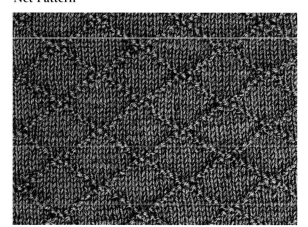

Can be combined with other patterns such as in top example on p.68.

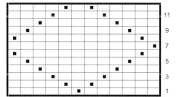

Pattern by Mrs Esther Nurse, Sheringham, about 1950

Vertical lines of diamonds and triangles, which are halved diamonds

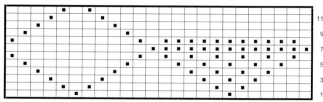

Large Diamonds and Herringbone, Leith (near Edinburgh)

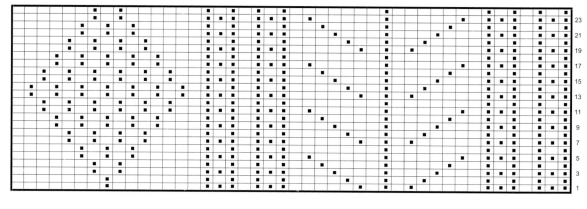

Pattern from Buckie and Mallaig

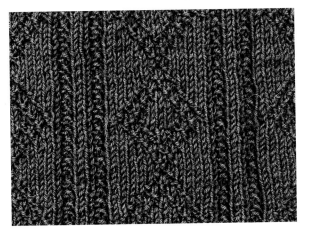

This diamond, called "heart in the home," symbolizes a good home atmosphere.

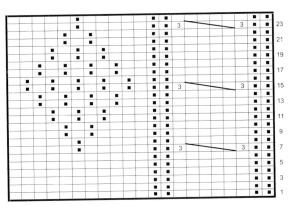

Cable and Big Diamond, Robin Hood's Bay

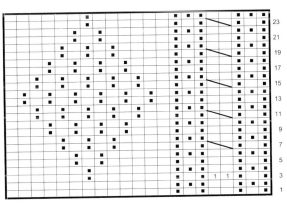

Big Diamonds and Mini Cable, Peterhead

Mrs Bishop's Pattern, Sheringham, about 1900

Herringbone with diamonds worked in Mary Ann's stitch

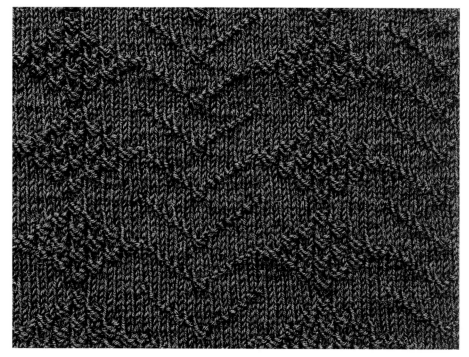

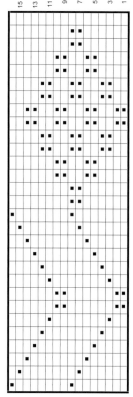

Scottish Fleet Pattern C

Line diamonds and small steps

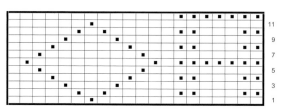

Vertical Patterns with Motifs—Herringbone

Herringbone Pattern from Polperro

Herringbone separated by narrow panels of Chicken's Eye pattern

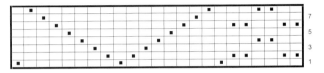

Wick Pattern with Herringbone and Small Chevrons

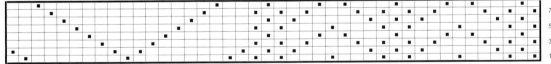

Herringbone and Mini Cable, Grampian Coast

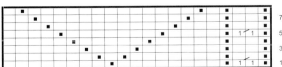

Vertical Patterns with Motifs—Zig-Zag

Lightning and Flash, Filey

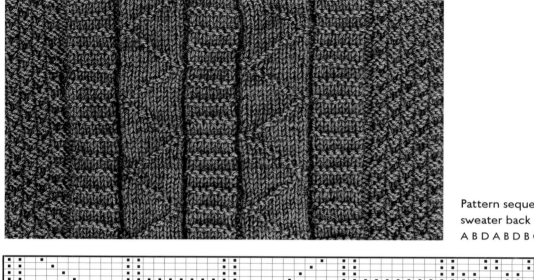

Pattern sequence across
sweater back or front:
A B D A B D B C B A C B A

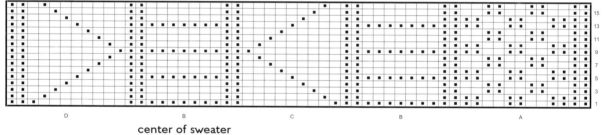

center of sweater

Scottish Fleet Zig-Zag Pattern

"Marriage lines" worked in 2 purl stitches

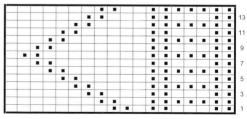

Zig-Zag Pattern from Grampian

"Marriage lines" worked in a 3-stitch Double Moss pattern

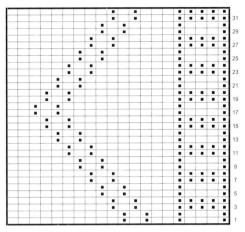

Arbroath Marriage Lines

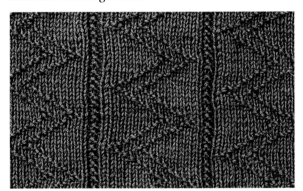

This pattern was worn only by married fishermen.

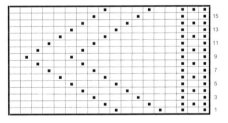

Zig-Zag Pattern from Boddam

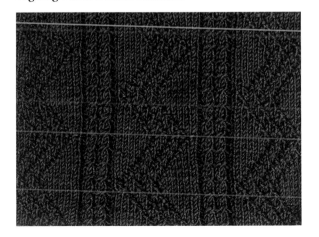

Mini cables with wide zig-zag worked in double moss stitch

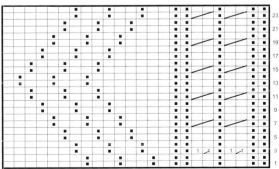

Zig-Zag pattern A from Wick

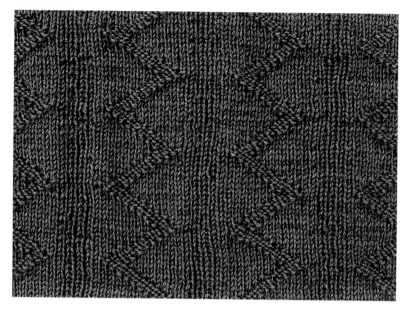

Opposite zig-zag lines separated by delicate rib patterns

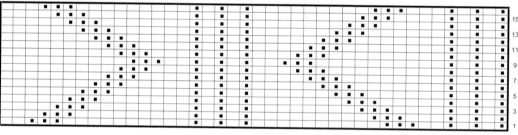

Zig-Zag pattern from Anstruther

This pattern with a 3-stitch purl zig-zag is taken from a sweater more than 100 years old, which was found in a loft and is now kept in the Scottish Fisheries Museum, Anstruther.

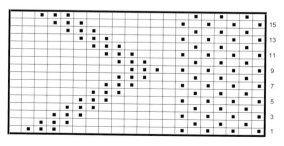

Zig-Zag Pattern B from Wick

The herringbone panel should be centered on sweater front and back.

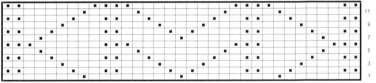

Zig-Zag Pattern by Mrs Rowe from Newbiggin (about 1980)

Wide moss zig-zag and tightly twisted cable

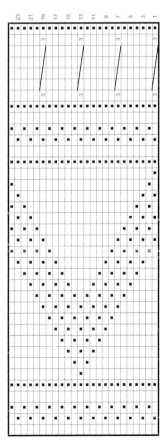

Vertical Patterns with Motifs—Steps, Ladders, and Bias Lines

Scottish Fleet Pattern D

Knit panels and short steps

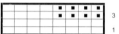

Sheringham Yoke Pattern

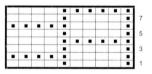

Grampian Steps

Checked pattern out of continuous steps

Step Pattern from Staithes

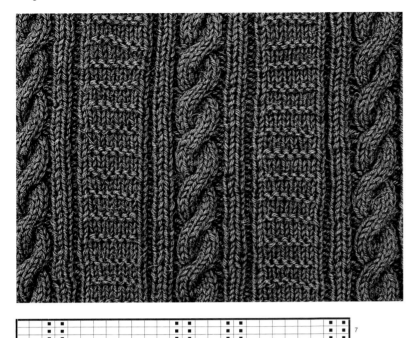

Cables, steps, and ribs

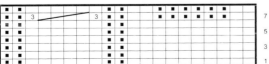

Filey Step Pattern

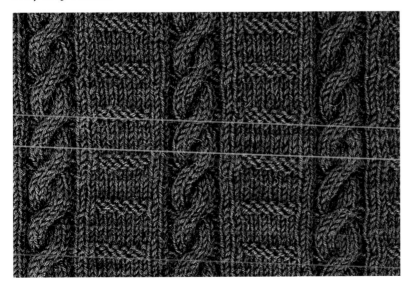

Steps and cable

Bias Lines from Arbroath

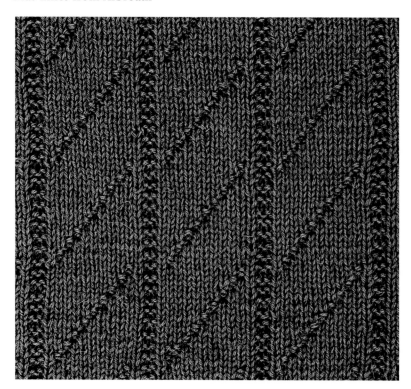

Bias lines are often called bars and stand for the sandbars near the harbor.

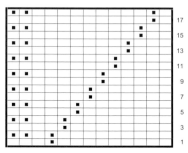

Scottish Fleet Triple Bars

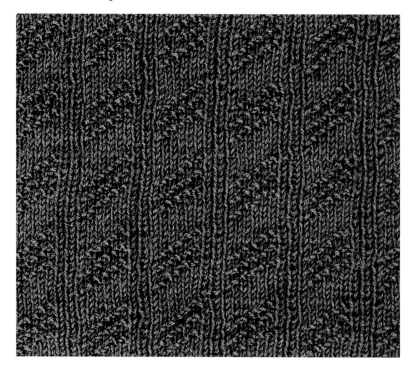

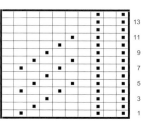

Vertical Patterns with Motifs—Tree of Life

Scottish Fleet Tree of Life A

Cable on moss background and boxed tree of life

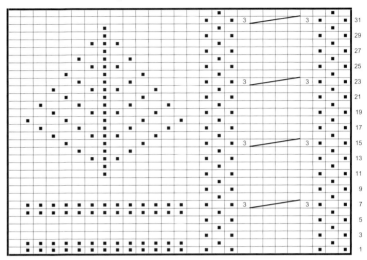

Musselburgh Pattern

Tree of life and cable on typical
Scottish background

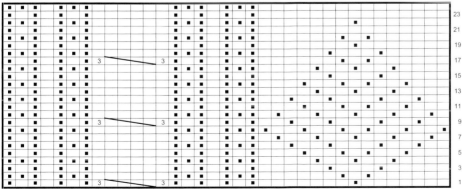

Grampian Tree of Life

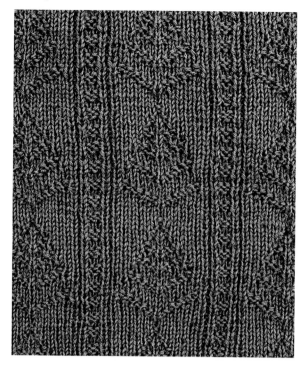

Tree of life with separating panel only found on Scottish patterns

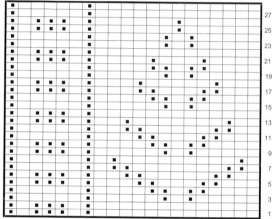

Anstruther Tree of Life (Scottish Fisheries Museum)

Extremely fine tree of life and separating panel of bias lines

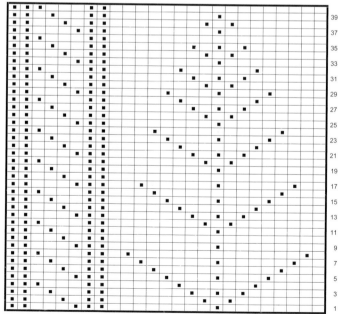

Scottish Fleet Tree of Life B

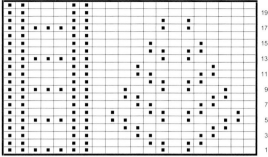

Mrs Laidlaw's Pattern, Seahouses

A very famous pattern that, around 1938, won a prize at a London craft exhibition

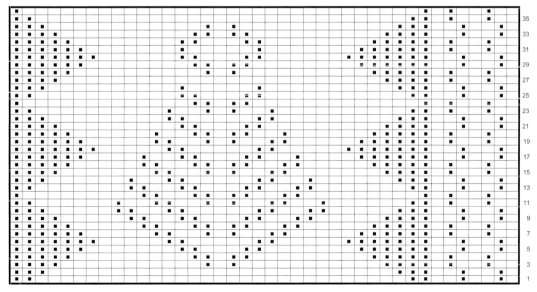

Vertical Patterns with Motifs—Triangles

Eddystone Pattern from Looe

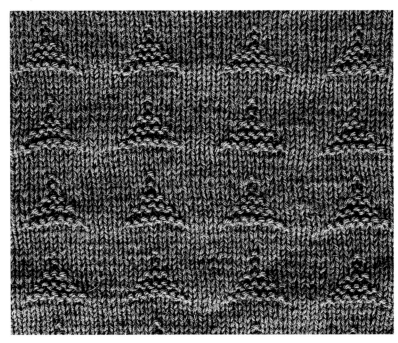

This pattern is named after the famous Eddystone Lighthouse off the coast of Cornwall. Originally worked only in the yoke.

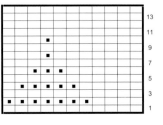

Caithness Flag Pattern

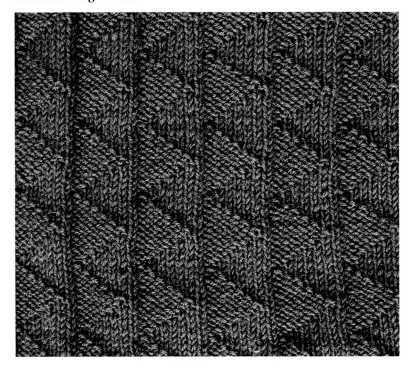

An attractive pattern with a pleated effect. For use in yoke, center on Stitch 1 of pattern repeat—the continuous knit stitch that separates the triangles. This pattern requires more stitches per inch than plain knit, so work an increase round before commencing the yoke: increase 1 in every 7th stitch. The added stitch becomes Stitch 8 of pattern repeat (the continuous purl stitch).

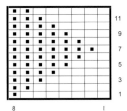

Scottish Half-Flag Pattern

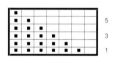

Scottish Fleet Flag Pattern

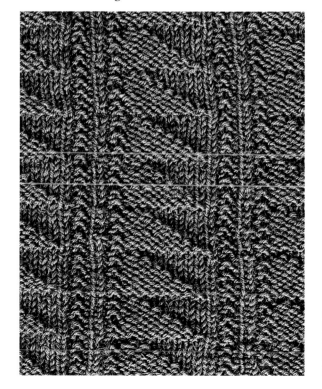

A typical Scottish separating panel runs between the columns of flags.

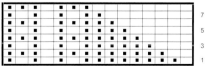

Vertical Patterns with Motifs—Chevrons

Scottish Fleet Chevron Pattern

Double moss chevrons between columns of steps

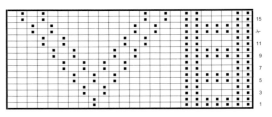

Chevrons and Ribs from Anstruther (Scottish Fisheries Museum)

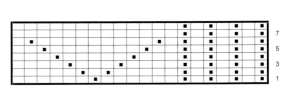

Chevrons, Ribs, and Steps from Inverness

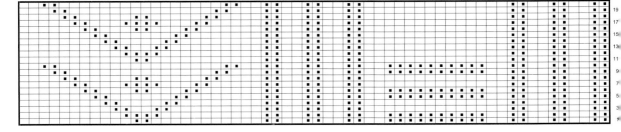

Complex Patterns

Filey and Flamborough

The patterns from Filey and nearby Flamborough are the highlights among the English fishermen's sweaters. It is impossible to show all possible variations. Therefore, it makes more sense to pick out the most important motifs, which can be varied in size and texture. Combined with cables of many kinds, and even with textured panels, and arranged according to one of the following formulas, the number of possibilities is really unlimited! This is the chance for a knitter to present her creativity and skills—at Filey, Flamborough, and elsewhere!

For designing a pattern of your own, take care that the repeats of all pattern elements are of the same number of rows/rounds or that the repeat of the longest is a multiple of the others. This makes knitting easier. The width of the individual panels may vary, which often looks rather attractive and even more lively.

Formulas for Vertical Patterns

The letter A stands for a cable or a textured separating panel, as seen on many Scottish patterns. Read these formulas in knitting direction, from right to left.

Center on A or B
A B A B A
(Example: Cable and Big Diamonds, Robin Hood's Bay, p. 69)

Center on A or C
A B C B A
(Example: Moss Diamond, Moss Panel and Cable, p. 87)

Center on A between D
A B A C A D A D A C A B A
(Example: Filey motifs, p. 88 top)

Center on D
A B A C A D A C A B A
(Example: Sweater in Filey Style, p.89)

Center on A between B
A B C A C B A B C A C B A
(Example: Gina's Pattern, p. 34)

Center on D
A B C A B C D C B A C B A
(Example: Margaret Taylor's Pattern, p. 89)

Pattern from Fisher Row (near Edinburgh)

Cable on textured background and diamond

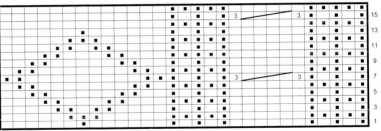

Pattern from Sennen Cove

Cable, moss diamond, and knit and gartered stripes

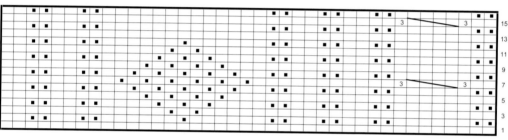

Flamborough Pattern

Cable, line diamond, and panels in moss variation

Pattern from the North Sea coast between Hull and Edinburgh

Very popular pattern consisting of Big Diamond, Betty Martin panel, and Cable

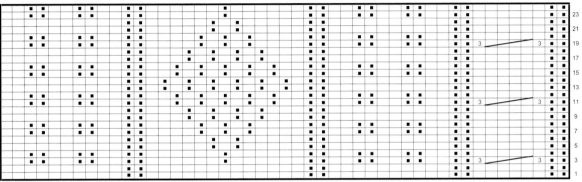

Flamborough pattern

Moss Diamond, Moss panel, and Cable

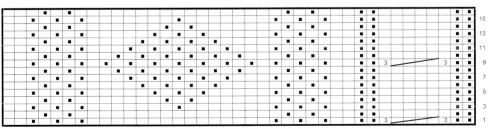

Filey Pattern Motifs A

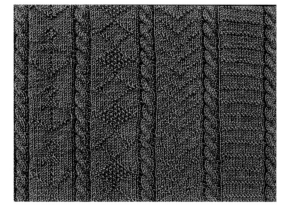

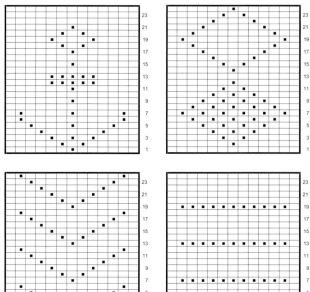

Filey Pattern Motifs B

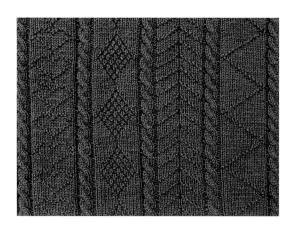

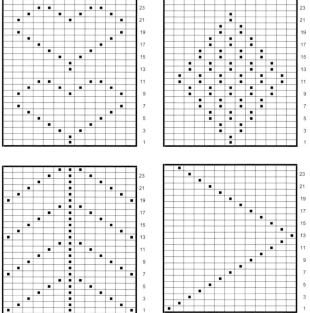

Margaret Taylor's Pattern, Filey

Center on column D. Motif sequence:
A B C A B C D C B A C B A

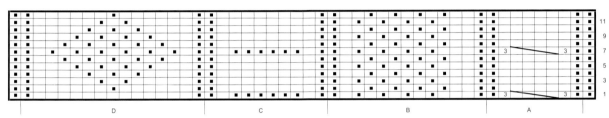

Sweater in Filey style

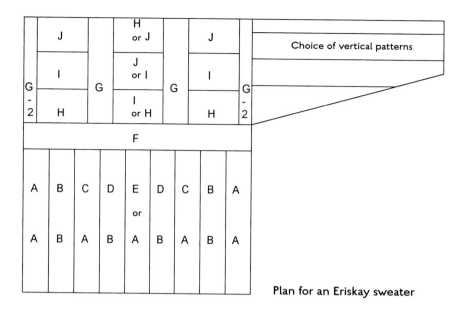

A	B	C	D	E	D	C	B	A
				or				
A	B	A	B	A	B	A	B	A

Plan for an Eriskay sweater

Eriskay

Of all fishermen's sweaters, the ones with the most complex patterns come from the Outer Hebrides off the west coast of Scotland. They were knitted on a small island called Barra and on even smaller Eriskay, where, since 1950, sweaters have been produced for sale. About 15 knitters started back then, but only two are left who still knit; the others have died or are too old. And, as is typical everywhere these days, the young people are not interested in preserving that heritage or in wearing hand-knit garments.

At first the patchwork of an Eriskay sweater looks rather confusing, but actually they are all constructed according to a clear geometric scheme. The number of motifs is limited; however, by interpreting the traditional elements in her own individual way, each knitter is able to create a new design with each new sweater—theme and variations!

For designing a pattern such as the one shown below, it is recommended to first knit a pattern sample large enough to comprise the center panel and one side panel in full length. Total width can be adjusted by modifying the separating panels; the panels along the armhole edges can be altered as shown here.

Ideally, all the motif sections in the yoke are the same height. At least the top and bottom ones should be identical in size. Don't forget to choose a horizontal pattern for the shoulder straps.

The yoke for an Eriskay pattern. See graphs on pages 92 and 93.

Original Eriskay sweater, knit by Margaret McInnes

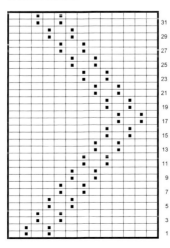

Here are some typical vertical patterns used for the circular-knitted part of front and back. Of course, any other vertical patterns may be used.

Starfish and Diamond

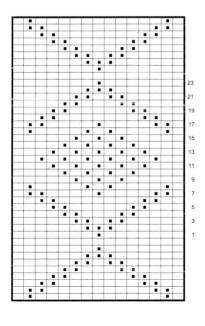

Wave Pattern

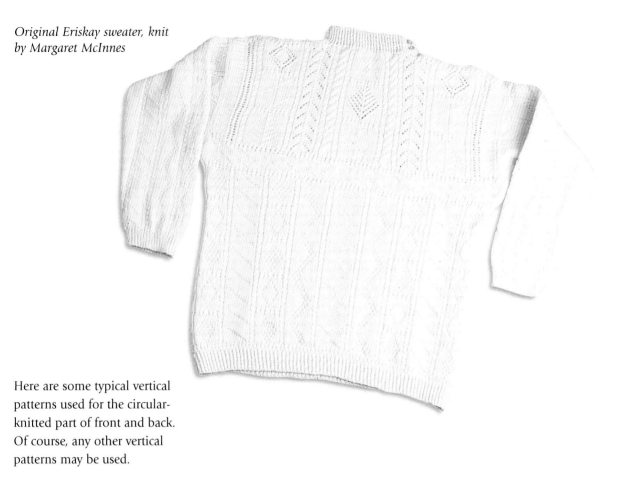

Small Starfish

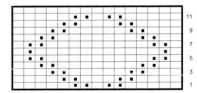

Eriskay Marriage Line

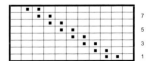

Chevron Pattern

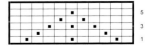

Here are two horizontal patterns often used for separating the vertical pattern of the body from the yoke. Horizontal chevron patterns such as those from Norfolk, Cullercoats and the Scottish fleet (pp. 60 and 61) are other preferred choices.

Traditionally, this band is bordered above and below by the so-called Indian Corn Stitch (see sidebar), which can also be used for a vertical border.

Single Net Pattern

Triple Net Pattern

Indian Corn Stitch

Work on an even number of stitches.

Row/round 1: Yarn round needle, knit 2, lift yarn over the 2 knit stitches so that the yarn is laid in front of them.

Rows/rounds 2 and 4: Purl in rows, knit in rounds.

Row/round 3: Knit.

When applied horizontally, work only rounds/rows 1 and 2; for a vertical border, work all 4 rounds/rows.

The photo on page 90 shows narrow bands of Indian Corn Stitch bordering the horizontal net pattern on the Eriskay layout.

Motifs for the Eriskay Patchwork Yoke (shown on pages 90 and 91)

Diamond Variations

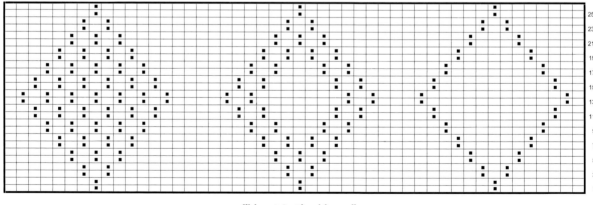

"Heart in the Home"

Starfish

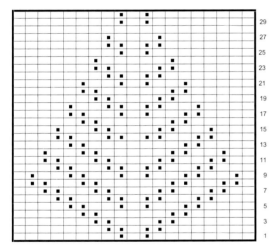

Tree of Life

St. Andrew's Cross

The pictorial yoke motifs are often knitted in **openwork technique:** Yarn round needle (YRN; also called a yarn over), knit 2 stitches together, then purl all stitches and the YRNs as you work back across on the wrong-side row. Position the YRN on the side of the first, lower purl stitch in each pair of purl stitches shown in the graphs (shaded in example below).

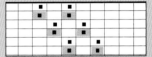

Vertical separators:
Cables of various kinds, combined with Indian Corn Stitch or openwork bands, just as you like.

More Pictorial Motifs

Anchor

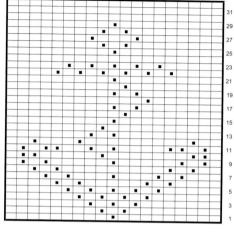

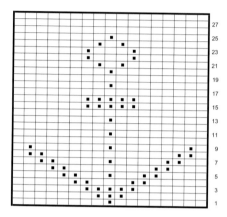

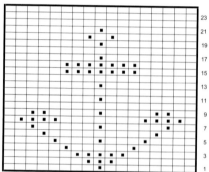

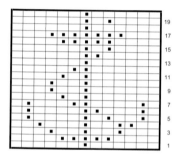

Heart

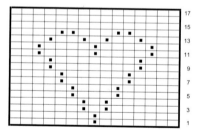

Cross

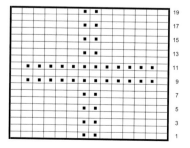

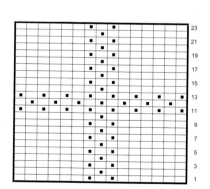

Initials

Of course, initials always have to be designed individually. As only a few letters are needed, it is not difficult at all to design one's own initials. A good position for initials is about three-quarters of the way to the side line of the sweater, as shown below.

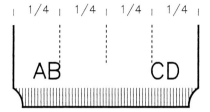

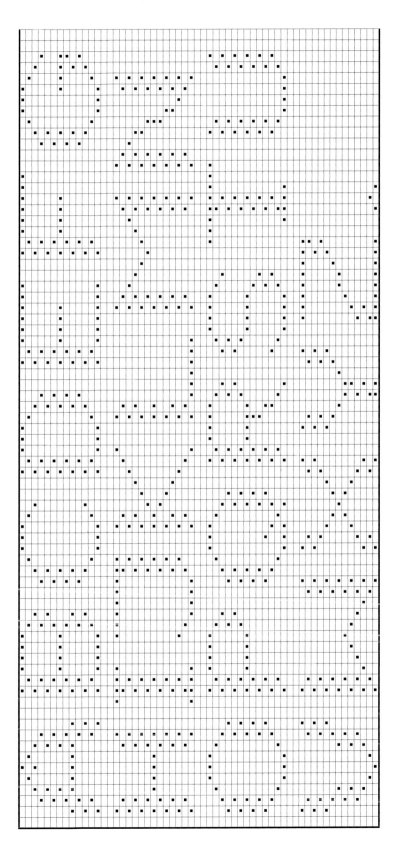

Yarn Sources

Traditional Guernsey wool can be ordered from **Frangipani Knitwear,** Janet Stanland, Meaver Farm, Mullion / Helston, England TR12 7DN. Tel. +44 (01326) 240128, Fax +44 (01326) 240011; *www .guernseywool.co.uk*; e-mail *frangipani@eclipse.co.uk*

Guernsey wool and fishermen's sweaters can be purchased from **Flamborough Marine Ltd**, Flamborough, Bridlington, England YO15 1PD. Tel. and fax: +44 (1262) 850943; *www.manorhouse.clara.net*; e-mail *manorhouse@clara.co.uk*

The following yarns also work well for traditional fishermen's sweaters and are available from many vendors. The Wool Works website—*www.woolworks.org/stores.ht*—is very helpful for locating yarn suppliers in your area.

• **Wendy Guernsey 5-ply, 100% wool:** 100 g (3.5 oz.) skeins, 224 m (245 yds); 28 stitches and 36 rows per 10 cm (4 in) on 2¼ to 3 mm (U.S. size 1 to 3) needles. Thomas B. Ramsden & Co., West Yorkshire, England; *www.tbramsden.co.uk*

• **Top of the Lamb sport weight, 100% wool:** 1.75 oz (50 g) skeins, 154 yds (142 m); 24 stitches per 4 in (10 cm) on U.S. size 5 needles. Brown Sheep Co., Mitchell, Nebraska; *www.brownsheep.com*

• **Heilo sport weight, 100% wool:** 50 g (1.75 oz.) skeins, 100 m (116 yds); 24 stitches and 28 rows per 10 cm (4 in) on U.S. size 3 to 5 needles. Dale of Norway; *www.daleofnorway.com*

Acknowledgments

Many thanks to all people who in some way contributed to this book!

Feine Handarbeitsnadeln, Gustav Selter GmbH, Altena, and Coats GmbH Salach (Schachenmayr knitting yarns and Gedifra) generously donated all tools and materials. Special thanks go to English and Scottish friends who helped with the research: Lesley Berry, Morag Campbel, Jim and Val Haxby, Jean and Malcolm Johnson, Margaret McInnes, Doreen Pickering, Gina and Richard Robinson, Janet Stanland, Margaret and Graham Taylor, Mary Wright, and Norah Woodhouse.

And last but not least, lots of thanks to my family—Uwe, Carsten, Marina, and Imke—for active contributions and constructive criticism, for joining the research travels, and for their great patience.

Books Consulted

Rae Compton. **The Complete Book of Traditional Guernsey and Jersey Knitting**. London, 1985.

Rae Compton and Henrietta Munro. **They Lived by the Sea**. Thurso, 1983.

James Norbury. **Traditional Knitting Patterns**. London, 1962.

Michael Pearson. **Traditional Knitting**. London/Glasgow, 1984.

Gladys Thompson. **Patterns for Jerseys, Guernseys & Arans**. New York, 1969.

Mary Wright. **Cornish Guernseys & Knit-Frocks**. London, 1979.

Photograph Credits

Pages 4, 24–51: Uli Staiger / die licht gestalten, Berlin.

Pages 8, 11, 14, 16, 21–23: Sabine Domnick

Pages 10, 17, 18, 19, 54–90: Carsten Domnick

Page 52: Scottish Fisheries Museum, Anstruther

Pages 53, 57 bottom: Royal Cornwall Museum, Truro

Page 58 top: Scottish National Archives, Edinburgh

Pages 13, 89, 91: Jane Wander im Hause Foto Walberg, Kappeln

Art Credits:

Knitting graphs: Marina Collet

Measurement diagrams: Gisela Klöpper, Coats GmbH, Salach

Page 6 map: Sabine Domnick

Pages 8, 9, 10, 14, 15, 16: Marina Collet

Pages 12, 18: Sigrid Witzig

Page 13: Susanne Nöllgen